E MON...
CAYTHO... CAMP...

...phone (01400) ...52...

UNDERSTANDING THE WORKING LURCHER

UNDERSTANDING
the
WORKING LURCHER

Jackie Drakeford

The Crowood Press

First published in 2000 by
The Crowood Press Ltd
Ramsbury, Marlborough
Wiltshire SN8 2HR

British Library Cataloguing-in-Publication Data
A catalogue record for this book is available from the British Library.

ISBN 1 86126 344 9

Dedication
For Phillip, who bravely welcomed lurchers into his previously quiet life.

Acknowledgements
Thanks are due to Colin Norman, Nigel Stentiford, Peter Marriage, Sarah Smith, Lana
Gazder, Jules Wettern, David Marr, Brian Plummer, Rob Moore, John and Karen Tredgett,
and Dave and Ali Lovatt for sharing their wisdom with me over the years; to Phillip
Blackman, Jo Lundgren, Rob Moore, John Tredgett, Angie Dear, John Dear and others for
their help with the photographs. Thanks also to the various lurchers, past, present and future,
who have given their speed and skill so willingly, and the many sporting landowners, farmers
and gamekeepers who have so freely and generously shared their land.

Typeset by Phoenix Typesetting
Ilkley, West Yorkshire

Printed and bound in Great Britain by
WBC Book Manufacturers, Mid Glamorgan

CONTENTS

Definitions		6
Prologue		7
Chapter 1	Choosing a Lurcher	8
Chapter 2	Training	26
Chapter 3	Entering to Quarry	57
Chapter 4	Fitness	88
Chapter 5	Permission to Hunt	109
Chapter 6	Care and Maintenance	118
Chapter 7	Lost, Stolen or Strayed?	129
Chapter 8	Breeding Your Own	135
Chapter 9	The Declining Years	166
Epilogue		172
Recommended Reading		173
Useful Addresses		173
Index		174

DEFINITIONS

Purists maintain that a lurcher is a cross between a running dog – greyhound, whippet and so on – and a working dog – collie, labrador and the like – whereas a longdog is a purebred running dog or a cross between them. I have used the terms interchangeably, as they are all 'long dogs'. Because most people prefer to hunt bitches, I have referred to the lurcher as 'she' throughout this text, but unless specifically mentioned, either sex is implied.

PROLOGUE

Why a lurcher? What is the attraction of these silent, remote dogs? It is as much what they are as what they do.

The lurcher has been with us for thousands of years. Large or small, rough or smooth, she appears on the walls of tombs, in paintings, tapestries and jewellery, on pottery, and has been lovingly modelled in every kind of stone and metal. She has been interred with her owner, so that her spirit and his may forever hunt together. She has been so dearly loved that her likeness has been commanded to surmount her grave. She has been as much a kindred soul and helpmate to the human hunter as the horse and the falcon, and there are a few places left on this earth where the four hunt together still.

She has been reviled as the poaching dog, the moucher's cur, her racy lines hidden under a shaggy coat. She is a thief, an opportunist: she comes, she goes, in silence. The landscape closes around her until she reappears, fur or feather in her long jaws. Nowadays, she who was once the hound of princes and chieftains, and then of the lawless, has no need to hide what she is. Equally at home in baronial hall or bedsit, she asks only kindness, warmth and the opportunity to hunt. Look at her: streamlined, graceful, powerful. Yet there is no aggression in her, only infinite gentleness.

You have perhaps seen the other side of her, the ultimate hunting machine, whether sifting the air to find hidden quarry, or full pelt at its heels, matching turn for turn before one final, decisive strike. Was it this that kindled your desire to have one of these beautiful dogs for your own? Did you go to the Dog Rescue to get something completely different, and were you then stopped in your tracks by a slender snout and huge, gorgeous eyes? Once you have shared your life with a lurcher, nothing else will do.

These pages will guide you through the ownership of your first lurcher, choosing, training, caring for and working her. Once you have mastered the basics, she and all the ones who come after her will teach you everything else that you need to know.

CHAPTER 1

CHOOSING A LURCHER

How would you like your lurcher to be bred? Different crosses have different characteristics and specialist talents, so it makes sense to have a good look at the differences before you finally decide which is the right one for you. Just as you choose your car for how and where and how often you plan to drive it, so your ideal lurcher will depend on the work you want her to do, the country over which you mean to work her, and your own temperament, which must be compatible with hers. When discussing the following crosses, I am assuming a 50 per cent cross, for example Collie/Greyhound = one parent Collie, one parent Greyhound, unless otherwise stated. If both parents are Collie/Greyhound, you will not get this 50 per cent cross, because genetics do not work like that. In this case, you will get a percentage of equal Collie and Greyhound genes, and a percentage of pups that are almost pure Collie or almost pure Greyhound. If C = Collie and G = Greyhound, the one-parent Collie, one-parent Greyhound will give pups as follows: CG, CG, CG, CG, and so on. If both parents are CG, the equation is CG + CG and the pups will be: CC CG CG GG and so on.

Bearded Collie cross, bred by David Hancock.

Another factor to take into account is that although each parent contributes exactly half of the genes, the pups are brought up by their dam only, and so will be inclined to take on a similar temperament to hers because they will copy her. It is the nature/nurture argument: although the pups have 50 per cent of their sire's temperament, they will follow their mother's example and adopt her ways. A laid-back Greyhound is very different from an exciteable Collie, so it will seem as if the pups have inherited their dam's temperament, when in fact what they are doing is learning behaviour from her.

The following descriptions of the more common crosses have, of necessity, been generalized, and you can only generalize about animals up to a point, after which they will gleefully make you out to be a complete idiot. Therefore, take these descriptions as guidelines only, for there undoubtedly will be dogs around that will prove me wrong in every case. However, these observations have been made over many years and many dogs, and are as useful as I can make them.

It is a wise dog that knows its father, and a lucky prospective lurcher owner that can be sure how his or her pup has been bred. Commercial lurcher breeders know exactly how their dogs are bred, and will in most cases be able to show you both parents, and even give a potted history of each. Many people breed from a favourite bitch in order to carry on the line, and will choose the stud dog with tremendous care. Some of these dogs will be 'pedigree unknown', their pedigree being in their working ability. Unfortunately some people will breed from anything in order to make money, but making money from lurcher pups is very difficult unless you either operate a commercial unit of a sufficient size to pay its way, or the pups and bitch are not done well. Beware of this last sort of person, or the dog dealer who just

Welsh Border Collie cross, hence the prick ears.

happens to have a litter of pups in (no dam) bred exactly the way you want. And if the next customer wants a different cross, they will be bred that way next. If you are buying in your first lurcher pup, you will be streets ahead if you buy from the commercial breeder with a reputation to maintain, or the home breeder with the one litter bred for own use and raised with unstinting care, rather than the fellow out to make a fast buck. Lurcher pups are much of a muchness at eight weeks old, though by six months, they will be revealing their breeding. Many a good sapling has been acquired from the Dog Rescue; indeed, I've done it myself, but if this is your very first lurcher, shop around and make sure that you get what you want. You are going to be together for as long as a good many marriages, so start off with a partner that you are going to get on with!

Border Collie/Greyhound

This is the classic cross, and probably one of the easiest to train for close work. This dog will be very biddable, have a good nose and coat, and will be hardy, long-lived and quick to mature. Border Collies nowadays can tend to have a questionable temperament, and many half-crosses have a snap in them, which needs to be remembered if small children or other dogs are about. Hybrid vigour (the enhanced good health of the crossbred compared to the purebred) means that the first cross is unlikely to manifest the hip and eye problems that plague the modern Border Collie, but with a half-cross to half-cross or more Collie, be careful. Likewise, the attractive merle colouring that is seen in some Border Collie crosses carries a sting in the tail: merle bred to merle creates a proportion of white pups that are deaf, blind or both, and sometimes also exhibit other serious abnormalities.

The Border Collie cross is a peach to train, and generally enters well into rabbit work. It is a good rough-terrain dog, with stamina to burn. Easy to feed and keep fit, most are natural retrievers and are very eager to please. First crosses are wont to stalk or round up their quarry, and so a lot of patience is required until the dog learns to use its mouth and actually pick up its quarry instead of just herding it towards you. They need encouragement to hunt, and must be tactfully entered to fox. Although good foxing half-crosses do exist, they are not the ideal cross for fox work, nor are they usually fast enough for hare coursing. However, once they have learned to hunt, they can be great opportunists, with a gift for being in the right place at the right time to lift a squatting hare or rabbit.

The Three-Quarters Greyhound One-Quarter Border Collie

This is bred with a Greyhound to a Collie/Greyhound, and is probably the ideal beginner's dog. Almost as easy to train as the half-cross, this dog is a better hunter and is game to tackle quarry that fights back (I know Collie/Greyhounds that won't tackle a rat or a squirrel, never mind a fox). These are good-looking dogs, for the most part with the sunny nature of the Greyhound, tough, early maturing, almost as long-lived as the first cross, and very forgiving of the novice owner's mistakes.

Border Collie/Whippet to Whippet.

The Reverse Three-Quarter Bred

This is the reverse to the above, where a purebred Collie is used on a Collie/Greyhound. Definitely a specialist dog, this one is hardy, well-coated, with good feet and excellent stamina. He is very easy to train in basic obedience and handling, but can be a reluctant to cowardly hunter, and definitely not for the newcomer to lurcher work. I have seen a number of these work, and have been unimpressed by their surly natures and lack of 'try', although I am assured that good ones do exist. It is a real 'moucher's' dog if you get a good one.

The Bearded Collie Cross

This is Mr Tough – heavy coat, great feet, grows fat on rations that would starve a Greyhound, goes on for ever and pretty near lasts for ever. That coat might be too hot in lowland areas, or too prone to balling in snow or mud, and will certainly need more than token care and maintenance. While not the easiest dog to train, he has an eye for the main chance and a very independent streak. Some resent the lead bitterly and can be hard to lead train, although very good to heel off it. The purebred Beardie has a kinder, if scattier, temperament than the intenseness of the purebred Border, but remember that his original job was to hunt away and face down some very wild and bloody-minded stock. The Beardie lurcher will therefore hunt on better than the Border, but can also be more bumptious. He is a clever dog, and may start to pick and choose his quarry.

The Beardie/Border/Greyhound

Sounds a good idea, with a quarter of each Collie to pass on the good qualities of each, and the Greyhound to inject speed, amiability and sweetness. However, unfortunately it does not always work out like that. I've seen some very good ones, and some absolute rubbish. If they are not over-hunted, they will work averagely well, and certainly they are very pretty.

The German Shepherd/Greyhound

This cross has a good weatherproof coat and stamina, is obliging to train and likes to work close. It can be a little heavy for some jobs, as the modern German Shepherd is a much bigger-boned beastie than the ones that were doing military work during the two World Wars. The exaggerated stifle bend, hip, eye and digestive problems of the German Shepherd make this dog a time bomb for breeding purposes, so if this is the cross for you, make sure that you both see and like the German Shepherd side of the arrangement, as their working lives can be shortened by health problems. A strong guarding instinct is manifest in this dog, which must be carefully directed. This cross can take a while to mature both physically and mentally, has a sensitive nature, and needs skilful training and entering. Not the fastest dog, not always the boldest, but will do his best for you once he is sure what you want. For people who prefer a low profile, this does not look very much like a lurcher. Put back to a Greyhound, the three-quarter cross is faster and less neurotic, and more suitable for the beginner.

The Whippet/Greyhound

Do not be deceived by the fragile appearance of this cross – this is one tough dog. One thing Whippets have in spades is courage, and Greyhounds are not short of it, so you have a small death-or-glory hound here. What they fail to catch on the straight they will pick up on the turn, and no quarry holds fears for them. Your

Bedlington / Whippet aged nine months. Unusual fawn colour; first crosses are usually blue.

problem will be to stop them self-entering far too early. Naturally a wide-ranging dog, plenty of work and patience on the obedience side is needed before this permanently primed weapon is unleashed. Their noses are plenty good enough for hunting-up and marking, and they are capable of doing most jobs well. They are exceptionally sweet-natured and clean to keep, but they need a lot of good food and careful conditioning for fitness. They need just that bit more care, for they are not stamina dogs, but they will try their hearts out, so you must be careful not to ask too much of them. Their coats and skins can be thin for cold or rough country and their feet tend to damage, not because they are weak but because these dogs go so fast. Their downside is the amount of trouble that their courage and speed get them into, and if you hunt rough terrain or barbed-wire country, make friends with your vet, or even consider marrying one!

The Bedlington Terrier/Greyhound

Another of the classic crosses, this is a brave dog with a very good nose and total commitment to hunting, which will on occasion exceed her commitment to you. Tough and quick to mature, she can be a handful to train and will work with you rather than for you. This dog will be no problem entering to quarry, will face the thickest of cover, and dig like a JCB (in your garden, too). Easy to feed and keep fit, she may be touchy with other dogs, and it will take a strong personality to keep upsides of her, though it is only her longing to hunt that leads to a difference of priorities between you. This is a good cross for any job, and will take readily to fox work. In fact, if you add Bedlington blood, you will have a fox dog whether you want one or not. This cross will almost certainly have a 'killing mouth'.

Son of the lurcher shown on p.12 bred to a Deerhound / Greyhound ˘ Whippet.

The Whirrier (Whippet/Terrier)

The foremost of these is the Bedlington/ Whippet, but any sort of terrier can be crossed with a Whippet to make a good lurcher. The Bedlington is favoured because it is a silent breed, and also because its racy lines suggest that there may be Whippet blood in there already. The result is a small, agile rabbit dog with a blistering take-off kick, and speed enough over 25yd to ensure that not many rabbits go much further. These dogs can go almost everywhere a rabbit goes, turn like you wouldn't believe, face cover like heroes, and will go to ground if you don't watch it. They are stubborn, fiery and determined, not always easy to train as they are far too bright for their own good, but trained they must be, for they have no idea of their limitations and will tackle anything.

The quality of this cross's coat and feet depends on the parentage: the Bedlington/ Whippet sometimes has a disappointingly linty coat, though by no means always, whereas a Border or Lakeland terrier would contribute a thick skin (in both senses) and a wiry coat. The Jack Russell cross can be very successful, too, though I would personally stay clear of the harder terriers such as the Plummer or Patterdale. There are those who consider that a whirrier cannot do anything better than a purebred Whippet, but in fact this is not so, for a whirrier has greater jaw power, bigger teeth, better coat and a real desire to work cover. Whirriers have nose to spare, and if your main work is bushing or ferreting, this cross is hard to beat.

The Deerhound/Greyhound

A super coat, long, strong feet and an amiable temperament characterize this cross. She is bold but not reckless, protective but not aggressive. The slowest of all the crosses to mature, physically and mentally, with a relatively short working

Saluki/Greyhound from a Rescue Home.

life, she will however take all legal quarry without hesitation. She requires infinite tact to train, for although she likes to please, she likes hunting more, and is exceptionally sensitive. Hers is not the hairtrigger response of the Collie cross, rather a dignified moment of consideration (too long for some people) before she elects to oblige. And oblige she will; it is just that she does things in her own time.

She is a touch on the large side for rabbit work, though these big dogs catch rabbits well enough. She has an excellent nose and is determined on her quarry: this cross makes a first-class fox dog as long as she has enough room, for not all deerhound crosses are as manoeuvrable as necessary for something that can dodge like a fox. And beware deer of all sizes, for you do not breed out hundreds of generations of deer-catching. The Deerhound cross will wed to her natural quarry above all others unless you put in some stringent training early on, and even then, it is unwise to be complacent. Deerhound crosses can be tricky to feed, tending not to be overly interested in food but having large frames to fill. She will be aloof with strangers, and her booming bay will protect your house nicely. Never fawning, even with close friends, she is nevertheless a very loyal dog, and one of the crosses that is affected very badly by a change of owner. A further cross to Whippet brings the size down to that of a good all-rounder; not so easy to find, but probably one of the best available.

Saluki/Greyhound

The Saluki has had a bad press and is supposed by some to be untrainable, but this is not so at all. However, she is hard work to train, because she is stubborn and sensitive. She will not forgive physical abuse, or any treatment that she perceives as unjust, and will simply down tools and refuse to co-operate. She needs firm but tactful handling and a great deal of affection. Like the Deerhound, she absolutely

Deerhound / Greyhound 'Lydia'.

blossoms as a house dog, and the more she is with you, the more she will be for you. She is not a dog that changes owners easily, but sadly one that often has to, because of this difficult temperament. The Saluki cross easily becomes withdrawn and distant if she considers herself maltreated, and situations that a Collie cross will barely notice will unravel her completely. However, when treated appropriately she is a fine, tough working dog, with legendary stamina, strong feet, hard bones and good coat. She is uncomplicated to feed, early maturing and has a long working life. She is deft on hares and deadly on foxes but may lose a few rabbits as she takes several strides to get into top gear. She has plenty of nose for ferreting and cover work, although her supreme talent is the long course over any terrain – she is as tough and agile as they come, though she never seems to hurry. I have heard few people speak well of the Saluki and Saluki cross, yet I know a man who works a purebred to all disciplines, and

she is without blemish. I have seen many Saluki crosses work, and they can do it all; whatever the pundits say, this is a useful stamp of dog as long as she is in the right hands. One warning though – stockbreak her early, and do the job well, for she has been bred since the dawn of time to hunt gazelle, and finds the thunder of retreating hooves tremendously exciting. She is a possessive guard dog as well and not afraid of anyone, so take care not to put her in the position where she may feel entitled to use her teeth, and so condemn herself to death.

The Gundog/Greyhound

One of my gamekeeper friends tells me that a 'keeper's lurcher always used to be a Flat-coated Retriever/Greyhound cross, and what a splendid-looking dog that must have been. Gundog crosses will have stamina, natural retrieving ability, good feet and tremendous nose, as well as the

Bull cross aged twelve months.

physical and mental characteristics typical of whichever breed of gundog has been used. Labrador first crosses tend to be big-boned and to have over-large heads, though there is a long-legged, snipey-faced subtype of Labrador that is rather frowned upon by the purists of the Labrador world, but which would make an attractive cross with a Greyhound. Labrador crosses are generally biddable and of course very versatile. The Spaniel crosses will hunt well, but will be that much hotter to handle, and the German Wirehaired Pointer is one hell of a dog in the right hands, and a 'heller' of a dog in the wrong ones – not for the faint-hearted, nor for the first-timer. The gundog crosses lack speed, but have stacks of drive and game sense, so if you get on well with gundogs, that stamp of lurcher could be the one for you. Suit your choice to your job: a wide-ranging grouse-moor sort of HPR (Hunt, Point, Retrieve) is not quite the thing for small fields, and a

Labrador cross will not make an outstanding lamping dog, though she will try her heart out for you. Some of the Continental breeds can be strong on foxes, but whether a Labrador or Spaniel cross would do that job would depend very much on the attitude of the parents (I know purebred Labradors that kill foxes). Beware the nose, though! You really do not need that amount of nose in a working lurcher, and if you have a deep-scenting dog that puts its nose down and heads for the hills, you will rue the day.

The Bull Terrier/Greyhound

This is usually the Staffordshire cross now that the first choice of Pit Bull is no longer available, but sometimes the English Bull Terrier is used. The Staffie makes the better cross because the breed is sounder; English Bulls are not bred symmetrically these days, being all head and

Kelpie/Border Collie to Whippet bred by Dave Sleight.

no quarters. What do you get for the Bull cross? A custom-made fox dog, with agility, stamina, good feet, strong jaws and tremendous courage. Many lurchers will take a fox now and then, but foxes are not easy, and to take them day in, day out, a dog needs total commitment to the job, indifference to being bitten, and a liking for combat. Once a lurcher masters the art of connecting with her fox without getting bitten, the kill will be over with great speed, but if she collects a nip while she is learning, she may never try again. This is not a problem with the Bull cross. Three centuries ago, Lord Orford crossed Bulldog (very different from today's crippled travesties) into his Greyhounds to give them fire, and it certainly did that, along with white chests and toes and the brindle colouring that we see nowadays. More recently, the Whippet had an outcross of Staffie blood for the same reason, and this influence can still be seen in the broad skulls and prominent eyes of many Whippets.

Bull Terriers and their predecessors, the Bulldog and the Bull and Terrier, were bred to be easy with people and aggressive with dogs, characteristics which are also evident in the half cross. The Bull/Greyhound can be too bold for her own good, for she will go full tilt at her objective without a care for what separates her from it in the way of rough going, wire or obstacles. Many fans of the Bull cross prefer the second cross (three-quarters Greyhound, one-quarter Bull), as these tend to have greater speed and elegance. The Bull cross is a happy dog, easy to keep as family and not difficult to train, but she has an override switch once she is launched, and therefore needs an owner with a lot of dog sense, and who has his or her wits about them.

The Cattle Dog Crosses

Here, I refer to the Australian Cattle dog, the Kelpie, and the Huntaway, all of which are used to drive the semi-feral sheep and cattle of Australia and New Zealand. Pest Controller Phil Lloyd and the famous bitch 'Speckle' are probably the best known of the Cattle Dog crosses, and the reason that we do not hear more of them is that they are very difficult dogs. Supremely talented hunters, they have a very strong guarding instinct and equally strong personalities. Lurcherman Dave Sleight works Kelpie crosses and Kelpie/Collies crossed to Greyhound and Whippet, and again produces excellent hunting dogs. With such dogs, bred and worked in a harsh environment, you have toughness and stamina, strong-mindedness, and a need to be both physically and mentally stretched every day. These are not dogs to be kept in kennels and only worked at weekends (if it isn't raining). These are not dogs to be left until they are a year old before training commences, nor are they for the dog-swapper. They are sensitive and loyal, and in the right hands make superb rabbit dogs, but they must be worked every day, and anyone taking on one of these must be as committed to training as they are to working their dogs. These dogs are not for beginners, and are very much a specialist lurcher.

The Bitza

Often spoken of with great scorn by the purists, the lurcher that is made up of 'bitza this' and 'bitza that' is very commonly met. You ask the owner how the dog is bred, and the answer goes something like: 'she's a Collie/Greyhound/

German Wirehaired Pointer cross aged twelve weeks.

Deerhound/Whippet/Bedlington . . .' and your eyes begin glazing over. Some people even add mathematics as in: 'one-eighth Border Collie, five-eighths Whippet . . .'. Genetics may be an exact science, but it does not split each pup into exact fractions of its component breeds. There is nothing wrong with bitza lurchers, and as long as you are aware that picking one is a lucky dip, you can have years of fun with them. People breed in multiple crosses for specific attributes, for example Deerhound for coat, Saluki for stamina, and Whippet to bring the size down. However, some pups will instead inherit coat from the Whippet, size from the Saluki and stamina from the Deerhound. But if you choose a bitza, you also have the perfect excuse for anything that goes wrong: 'Ah, well, that's the Saluki in her . . .'.

The Purebred Running Dogs

A look at the foundation crosses of our lurchers is also useful. The Greyhound is the foremost cross, the ultimate running dog, easy and cheap to obtain thanks to racing and coursing, both of which sports ensure that only the best are bred from. There is an enduring rumour that Greyhounds are 'stupid', which of course is nonsense. However, many Greyhounds are reared in circumstances that result in them being under-socialized in the vital early months of their lives. Any dog raised with minimal human contact will not be as easy to train as those who have been closely involved with humans from birth. Greyhounds that are reared with plenty of human contact are biddable and bright, and will train on as well as any lurcher. They are brave in the field, have plenty of 'nose' (there goes another old rumour), and a sweetness of nature that makes their company a delight. However, they do not have a great deal of stamina, their coats and skins do not offer much protection, and because of their tremendous speed, they get into more trouble than a slower dog would, both with collisions and toe damage. They are exceptionally

Half-sister to the lurcher shown on p.19 aged eleven months.

effective fox catchers, good lampers as long as you don't want to be out all night, possess sufficient nose and concentration to be good ferreting and bushing partners, and it hardly has to be said that if cours-ing is your game, a Greyhound can do it!

The Whippet is generally assumed to be more biddable than the Greyhound, but Whippets tend to have a great deal more socialization than most Greyhounds. Bold and fiery, the Whippet is a lock-on missile to any form of quarry, and must be watched so that she does not take on too much. Whippet crosses are used to bring the size down in lurchers, and a Whippet can turn with her quarry so closely, can leap and snap a bird out of the air or pull a rabbit out of a hole with such skill that I wonder more people do not use this agile little dog. Whippets are not just transistorized Greyhounds, but a very ancient breed in their own right. Like the Greyhound, they have sweet and gentle natures, are apt to injure themselves with their incredible speed, and have thin coats and skins. The acceleration of the Whippet is such that many scoop up rabbits without even turning them, and they are deadly on rats and squirrels. They will tackle foxes without hesitation, although they sometimes lack jaw power. The Whippet makes a greater contribution to the lurcher than simply reducing the size, and you get a lot of dog in a small package.

Where and for What?

When you decide which lurcher is best for you, give some thought to the quarry and the land that you will be working. For most lurcher owners, the primary quarry is rabbit, and rabbiting permission is much more easily acquired than any other. But are you going to work small fields, woodlands, large fields, moorland or downland? Is the land open, stock-fenced, dry-stone walled, hedged or drained by dykes? Is the soil sand, gravel, peat with rocky outcrops, heavy clay, chalk or flint? Will you be on heather, pasture or arable? Is the weather bleak and hard where you live? Can you let your dog hunt freely, or will you be forever limited by roads, railway lines or hostile neighbours? Will you need to be able to call your dog off or back to you whatever runs in front? All this should influence your decision, for lurcher types that excel in some areas will be disappointing performers in others. And then you must be honest about your own situation: will you be able to work the dog daily or weekly; will you be willing to spend ten minutes a day on training; do you have a friend or family member available to help you out if you are ill or have to work late; do you have a helpful vet and can you afford the bills? A high-maintenance dog may not be for you, or you might willingly put in the extra work for the extra performance. Only you can decide, and you and the dog must suit each other.

Gender Matters

Do you want a dog or a bitch? For some people it doesn't matter, while for others it is very important. A mixed household can be wearing when bitches come into season, unless either bitch or dogs can be sent away to a reliable temporary home until the season is over. Several bitches together will come into season consecutively, which can be very stressful on the males, and a bitch just past her season will still smell very alluring to male dogs. Spaying or castration offers another option, though it is bitterly disappointing to have done this and then to find that that animal which cannot be bred from is the best you have ever owned. It does not, however, affect working ability at all. If you do run a mixed group, the most natural way is several bitches and one dog. This will avoid the fighting that is likely with several dogs and even one bitch, which is fortunate as bitch fights are usually much nastier than scraps between dogs. Better have no fights at all, and keep to a single-sex regime. Bitches are generally preferred over dogs as they are more single-minded with regard to their hunting, and bitches will work with a fury and tenacity that is not always seen in dogs. However, male dogs can also make very good workers, and tend to be less complex in temperament than bitches.

Where From?

Unfortunately, Dog Rescues are bulging with lurchers, but most can be retrained to make good working dogs. Generally they are there through no fault of their own; most are still under two years old, for that is when the young lurcher is at her most wayward. Usually, they are guilty only of doing puppy things, such as chewing or digging, or they have learned to run away and not come back to the disagreeable, red-faced and shouting human. Some have been tried too early and will not chase –

these you can work with, but, sadly, not those who have been worked too early and damaged physically. Leave those for the pet homes. Many Dog Rescues can be reluctant to rehome dogs into a working environment, which is galling when you consider how healthy and happy most working dogs are. However, the Dog Rescues seldom see this side of things, and they do see many badly treated and dumped dogs. Handle the matter with your usual superb tact: once the Dog Rescue sees that you are offering a caring, permanent home, that is the extent of its remit, and what happens afterwards is up to you. Give them a decent donation if you possibly can, and then they can save some more lurchers.

Prefer a pup from a breeder? There are professional kennels and homebreds to choose from, but keep clear of dealers. Kennels with a reputation to maintain will provide you with a pup whose breeding is exactly known, and will tend to specialize in one particular sort of cross. A

Another view of the bitch shown on p.20. Note the growth plates on the front legs.

look through the classified pages of *The Countryman's Weekly* will find you Bedlington, Deerhound, Saluki and Collie crosses, each from establishments that breed nothing else. The private home can be every bit as good, a one-off litter bred 'for own use' being certain to come from stock that is well tested in the field. The litter may be what some would call 'mongrelized', in that there may be a number of different breeds in the cross which will result in an uneven litter, but an uneven litter is not a faulty one. In fact, it gives a wider choice to buyers, who may be sure that the parents were carefully chosen.

A professional kennel owner's dogs are unlikely to have been worked to the degree that is common in the parents of the one-off homebred litter. The various tasks involved in running a commercial outfit may leave the professional breeder too busy to work his or her dogs, which in any case are simply too valuable to be put at risk. However, this is not necessarily detrimental, because if a dog is the right shape and temperament it should be able to work, given correct entering. Some abilities, such as retrieving, a soft or a killing mouth, quarry sense and a willingness to tackle fox, are definitely inherited, and the homebred owner will have a much sounder idea of what his or her pups *will* do, as distinct from what they *should* do. You pays your money and takes your choice.

Which Litter?

When you go to see those litters of pups, the most important thing to look for is that they have been properly socialized. This does not mean mercilessly pulled around by small children, but a careful, supervised introduction and exposure to humans, other dogs, household noises, and so on. Pups shut in a shed for the first few weeks of their lives will never fully make up this bad beginning, and will be that

Nothing wrong with white dogs – a very useful Deerhound / Greyhound to Whippet.

much more difficult to train, and may be shy of loud noises or new experiences. Three to nine weeks old is a critical time in the development of a pup; if they have lived in isolation during that period, they will never reach their full potential. Look for friendly pups that come to you wagging their tails, and that react with pleasure to the human voice, welcoming your hands and trying to lick your face. Look for the breeder who has clearly spent time with the pups, knows their individual personalities, and quizzes you about the home that you are offering. Strong, healthy, well-adjusted stock will come from such a start, and be well worth their price. Incidentally, most breeders like to receive feedback about their stock, and will be pleased to hear occasionally how you are getting on.

Indoors or Out?

Do you intend to keep your dog in the house or in a kennel? There are 'fors' and 'againsts' each method, depending on so many outside factors. If you have a young family, the dog is often better in a kennel while you are training, for one wild game of chase or tug-of-war will destroy your retrieving programme. But lurchers love to be part of a family, and the more time you spend with them, the better will be the understanding between you. A dog in the house means more mess, mud and dog hair, but the dog has more chance of being better cared for if she is with you all the time, for you will see at once if she is unwell or uncomfortable. A dog idly stroked is a dog where thorns, lumps or ticks are found sooner rather than later. A kennelled dog may be out of the way, safe from tradespeople leaving the gate open and unable to steal or damage anything in the house, but she will also be unable to guard the house and will make an easy target for thieves. House or kennel, only you can decide, because only you can weigh up the differing factors involved in your particular set-up.

Which Pup?

You have decided on breeding, gender and accommodation, found a suitable litter of pups, and now you have to choose between these beguiling little whelps who have not yet achieved their lurcher streamlining, and could be almost any breed. In which case, what do you look for? For many people, the choice is instant, and as far as they are concerned there is only one pup in the litter. Go with this instinctive choice, for it will always be right. Sometimes, however, the choice is harder, and a good breeder will let you spend as long as you need with the pups, or even visit several times, before you make up your mind. One family videoed their children with a litter that I bred, and when they watched the video at home, realized that one particular pup had dominated the film, and that he was the one for them. As this was the pup that I had thought best for them as well, I was delighted. Whether sitting with the pups or filming them, you will see the bold pup, the shy pup, the one that sits away from the others and thinks things out, the one that gets on your lap, and the one that curls up on your foot. Each is right for somebody; you know your own temperament and circumstances, and you will know which pup will best fit into your world.

What about colour? A lurcher doesn't catch rabbits with her colour, so it will not affect her working ability, but it may well be a matter of importance to you. That dog and you are going to be a team, so you may as well get a colour that you like, because you will be looking at it for years. White, pied and black dogs show up over long distances, whereas wheatens, greys and brindles tend to camouflage. There is a prejudice against white lurchers, chiefly, I suspect, because they show up so well. It is said that they 'spook the quarry', but the inference is that they are more likely to be seen by other people, and hence are not for the person who poaches. I work a white bitch from time to time and she is almost luminous, but her catch rate is every bit as good as that of her more discreet colleagues. After dark, a black dog is in fact more easily seen than a white one. White dogs may be a little more delicate in their skins and nails than coloured dogs, but this is not invariably the case. I never mark colour at all when judging lurchers in the ring, for it just is not important to me. If, however, there are colours that you dislike, then don't get a dog so coloured. She deserves better than that, and someone else will find her beautiful.

CHAPTER 2

TRAINING

There are two phases to lurcher training, one being everyday basic obedience and the second being field training. For the first, you need your dog to come to you when you call her, sit or lie on command, stay when told, and walk to heel on or off a lead. These skills will see a pet dog comfortably through her life, and indeed are more than many pet dogs are ever taught, but your lurcher needs far more. She must jump an obstacle or go through it, enter water or cross it, be absolutely steady to domestic livestock and whatever else you do not want her to tackle (if you are working keepered land, for instance, you will want her to leave pheasants alone), stop when told, drop to 'down' at a distance, leave quarry, food or other dogs upon the command 'leave it', and retrieve. It is useful if she will change direction when hunting-up, so that you can direct her on quarry that you can see and she cannot. Most of this is straightforward as long as you remember that the dog is a sentient being, not a clockwork toy, she cannot speak English or any other human language, and you never get 100 per cent in anything.

Alert and willing to please.

The Fundamentals

To teach your dog to obey, you must be absolutely honest and consistent with your words. The dog associates one word with one action, but many of our words alter with context, which cannot be grasped by a dog. For instance, the dog is on the sofa. You say, 'Get down off that sofa you naughty dog, you know you aren't allowed on there!' The dog hears a babble of angry sounds, the only word of which she recognizes is 'down', but she is already lying down. You continue: 'Get down, you bad dog, look at those muddy pawmarks, GET DOWN NOW!' She can hear that you are angry and would like you not to be angry. She wants to obey you. You are telling her 'down', but she is already down. She might hunch down even further, she might wag her tail in appeasement, she may wet herself with fright. But she won't get off the sofa because you haven't told her to; you've told her 'down' and she is, yet you are still angry. You drag her off the sofa and give her a telling off, so now you have a bewildered dog and have sown the seeds for future disobedience because as far as she is concerned she is being punished for obeying the 'down' command. Next time, she won't be so keen on obeying that one, because it leads to a scolding.

What you must bear in mind is one word, one action. It does not matter what that word is, so long as you use the same word when and only when you want to produce that action. For instance:

- Sit = sit down. If, however, you say 'sit down', the dog does not know whether you mean 'sit' or 'down'.
- Down = lie down.
- Off = get off (the sofa, the chair, the vicar).

- Come on = come here.
- Stay = stay where you are. I will come back to you.
- Wait = stay where you are. I am going to give you another command.
- Get in = get in the car.
- Out = come out of (the field, the barn, the neighbour's flowerbeds).

Because you will be working your dog, it is useful to train her to obey hand signals. Again, be consistent. Here are a few that I use, which are pretty standard:

- Hand raised sharply, forearm bent = sit.
- Hand lowered sharply, arm straight = down.
- Arms raised in V above head = come here.
- Hand extended, palm out = stay.
- Tap thigh twice = heel.
- Sweep arm to right or left = this way.
- Sweep arm forward = get on and hunt.

Along with the hand signals, I have a few whistle signals. I like my dogs to come here, stop and turn to a whistle signal, and later I will teach them one particular whistle that means they should look on the ground for a squatter. Make sure that these whistles are quite different from each other. However, if you plan to take your lurcher beating or picking-up, be aware of the confusion and whistle-deafness that may result from an environment where a lot of people are giving whistle signals to a lot of dogs. This can ruin all your training, as lurchers are such sensitive dogs. I would recommend that you use only your voice in these situations.

If you want your dog to respect and obey

you, then you must be honest with her. Don't call her to you and then punish her, whatever the crime, as she will associate coming to you with being punished. (There goes your recall training.) Don't cheat her by giving a 'squatter' whistle when there is no squatter. Don't allow other people to tease her by giving cries of 'rats' and the like in an excited voice. Never, ever be dishonest with a dog, particularly if you want a successful hunting dog, because shortly after she learns that you can't be trusted, she will also learn not to respect you. My dogs know that certain sounds mean that quarry is on the move, and they will come to me at full pelt because they know that I never lie to them. They ignore anyone else's orders, and only my trusted hunting partners know their hunting vocabulary.

One more command that I find useful is to teach the dog to empty herself when you want her to, for example after a long car journey and before you go into someone's house. Pick a command that doesn't readily come up in everyday conversation (the Woodhousian 'hurry up' and 'quickly' are far too hazardous!) and that you can comfortably use in delicate company. I would not suggest taking it to the point that the dog is only to empty herself when you say, but it is handy for both of you to know what you have in mind when you lead her up and down the same stretch of grass.

Generally speaking (and there will always be exceptions) a pup will be eager to obey you up until about six months of age, when it would normally be very much under the dominance of its dam. Then she will go through a bolshie stage which will last from a few weeks to the best part of a year, during which you will be sorely tried. This is one of the main reasons that the Dog Rescue societies have so many sapling lurchers. Many really good dogs go through this, so if yours is one of them, be patient, for it will certainly get better – but you will have to put the work in. Don't be too proud to go to obedience classes, for they will prove to be a good discipline for both of you. Your dog will learn to obey

Amphibious training.

you despite the distractions of other dogs, and you can take comfort on seeing dogs far worse behaved than yours. When you work in isolation it can be easy to think that no-one else has had any problem in training their dog, but that is far from the truth.

When attending a class, choose your instructor carefully, for like all professions, standards vary. The vigorous approach that may be suitable for a Rottweiller or Labrador will be totally wrong for a sensitive character like a longdog. Always watch a few classes to assess whether this is the instructor for you and your dog before you part with any money. A good rule of thumb is to see how the 'down' is taught. If the dog is thrown or in any way forced to the ground, avoid this class. Also remember that long-backed dogs find the 'sit' position uncomfortable and prefer to lie. If your instructor is not flexible enough to accommodate this, find one who is. I can call to mind four excellent dog trainers who are very different people: one is a gamekeeper, one a poacher, one an academic, and one a gundog field trialler. You would not meet such varying characters under one roof, but all have in common that they are quietly spoken, consistent and receptive to new ideas.

Ten minutes of training a day is better than one hour once a week. Lurchers like to please, but are generally unmotivated by food, so you may find titbit training, which is the current fashion, does not provide much incentive for them. Therefore you must bond strongly with your dog, so that you are the highlight of her day. After all, why should she please you, when with considerably less effort, she can please herself? You and only you must be the source of all things good, and your authority must be absolute. Never negotiate with a dog – this is interpreted as weakness. If a training exercise is showing signs of going horribly wrong, step back to an exercise that she does well, reward her, and call it a day for that session. If she performs a new exercise well, praise and

Steady to cat.

reward her lavishly, and end the lesson right there. Always quit while you are ahead. Rare is the human that can concentrate for longer than ten minutes, and rarer still the dog, so keep your training sessions short. Don't train when you are out of temper or in a hurry; you will also find a hungry dog more receptive than a fed one. Finally, don't underestimate the value of the lead as a training aid (and I don't mean sharply applied to the dog's quarters, no matter how much you may long to). The lead is a tangible link between the two of you, the promise of an outing, and the relaxation of mental control when you are not feeling up to it. If your authority is being challenged for whatever reason, put the lead on the dog, and the pressure is lifted from you both. Obedience is a habit, disobedience too, and the lead reinforces your control of any situation.

There are dog trainers who recommend that a dog should be kennelled away from you, so that when you release her for training, she will be much more eager to respond to you. Then there are those who saturate a dog with their presence, so that she bonds as strongly as possible with her handler, tucked into a shirtfront as a tiny pup, in the car with them, following them around the house, possibly even sleeping on the bed with them. Both methods work. Each, however, suits a particular type of dog: a dominant dog that is constantly with her handler may well nurture ambitions of moving up in the pecking order, and in family situations will often consider herself above every human except her handler (and he'd better not show weakness). A gentler dog, or, curiously enough, one of those maddeningly self-contained jobs that never play, never lose their cool and rarely show affection, benefit enormously from a secure place within their human pack that includes maximum involvement in the day-to-day trivia. These latter, in a kennel environment, will cease to relate to anyone or anything, and withdraw completely. Bombarded with stimuli, they eventually begin to respond, and, difficult though they may be, will

Steady to sheep.

often become sterling companions. Certainly, the people I know who have superbly trained Saluki crosses (and, in one case, a purebred show Saluki) spend every possible moment with them, whereas big critics of these sensitive dogs tend to be the sort who keep a dog in a kennel all the time that they are not training or working her. I strongly suspect that the so-called intractability of the Saluki relates to kennel-kept dogs that simply give up and refuse to respond to their jailers. Equally, I know of boisterous collie and gundog crosses that easily get too big for their boots and benefit from a spot of solitary.

While training, do not kennel your dog with another dog, for she will then bond with that other dog rather than with you, which lays the foundations for trouble later. This is especially so when you breed from a favourite bitch and run the pup on with her dam. The dog pack is not a random collection of canines that met in the woods one day, but a family group, and the pack that is created with a mother-and-pup combination is the strongest and most difficult unit to break up. Break it up you must, if you are to remain in charge of these two. Yes, the dam will teach the pup useful things like coming when she is called, how to find quarry, how to work cover, enter water and so on, but she will also teach it that the two of them are faster than you, and that her company equals more fun than yours. Two lurchers who are used to working together form a lethal team and, while this is desirable when both are trained, if you let that team develop before you are truly on top of the youngster, your old bitch will become unsteady, your youngster unruly, and the pair of them a living nightmare. Does this sound like the voice of experience? It most certainly is, so learn from my mistake and do not run a pup on with her

Steady to ferret.

mother! Train the sapling separately, bringing them together when the youngster has learned steadiness. You will still have a lethal working team, but they will be working for you rather than each other (you may as well tag along, if you can keep up). If you have already let the bond form, and are having troubles, it can all be cured, but it takes time. Separate them totally – exercise and feed them separately, and do not let them sleep in the same place, and they will each start to come back to you. If you walk them together sometimes, then one on the lead and one off is the routine, never both off together, while endeavouring to ensure that each dog has one-to-one time with you. Divide and conquer is true of any pack or herd beast, us too, and you will win this one if you are prepared to work at it.

There are only three ways of training: punishment and the absence of punishment; pleasure and the absence of pleasure; and the conditioned reflex (habit). If you ever doubt the power of the conditioned reflex, ring a bell in the presence of a fireman and watch him spill his beer.

We use a mixture of these methods nowadays. Dogs used to be trained almost wholly by the punishment method ('First break the dog – then train it'), but now we use pleasure and habit to reinforce behaviour patterns, with punishment as a last resort. Most animal training is kidology, in that you arrange a situation where the animal does what you want it to do because that is the most pleasurable course of action open to it and therefore what it wants to do as well. Then you reward it for doing what you both want, and so establish the behaviour. This is what, in trendy business courses, is called a 'win/win situation', that is, I win (you've done what I want), dog wins (has been rewarded for doing what it wanted to do). So what happens when you pick up a lead and get started?

Lead Training

Although most lurchers lead-train without fuss, some will fight it, with the dog pulling back or throwing itself down screaming and generally behaving as if it thinks you are about to hang it. This takes time and patience to tackle, so if you are short on either, do not train on that particular day.

If you have another dog, you can sometimes kid the pup into walking with her lead threaded through the collar of the other dog. Incidentally, don't introduce your dog to collar and lead on the same day; familiarize her with the collar right from the beginning. When first you put the lead on, call her to you once the lead is on, and make a big fuss of her when she comes to you. Never jerk her towards you on the lead, and don't take hold of her collar in anger, for she will see to it that you do not get another chance. Do, however, handle her collar and neck often, so that she realizes that your hand on her collar means nothing fearful.

Back to that pup, straining away from you at the furthest end of her lead. Can she be jollied along with a favourite toy or a titbit? If not, for a few days, that lead will be on her all the time that you are there to supervise. You will lead her to her food and water, and leave a short end of lead on her collar so that she feels the drag of it constantly, but only when you are there to ensure that she does not get caught up. Will she follow once you drop the lead? Many lead-haters walk beautifully to heel off the lead, which may tempt you to bypass this exercise, but please persist. What happens if you just sit down and wait? Eventually, (you may need the company of a good book – this could take some time) a sad pup will come up to you. Welcome her, give her a cuddle and read a couple more pages of your book before moving to the end of the lead, and sitting down again. I took on a pup that spent nine days screaming and fighting the lead, but by giving her nothing to fight and nothing to shriek about, I eventually won, though goodness knows what all that sitting on cold pavements did to me. It is exasperating when a pup won't walk on the lead, but she is fighting from a desperate, primitive fear of the thing around her neck, so summon up some understanding along with your patience, and give her time to trust you.

It is unusual to have a lurcher that pulls on the lead – they are usually far too dignified – but if one does, this is easily corrected. I carry a spare lead and swing it from side to side in front of the dog's nose as I walk, or choose narrow places that give her no option but to stay behind. The 'tramlines' across arable fields are useful, if you have a friendly farmer. Some trainers stop dead or turn away as soon as the dog tightens the lead, which is usually quite sufficient for lurchers, though more rumbustious dogs such as terriers will push their owners until they receive physical discipline, such as a tap on the nose or even, in extreme cases, the choke chain. If it is your intention to do Kennel Club Obedience, where the dog is required to walk with its head across your thigh and maintaining eye contact with you, sitting every time you stop, then the foregoing will not be of use to you, and I would suggest that right from the beginning, you use a trainer who specializes in this highly ritualized style of performance. I would also recommend that you do not buy a lurcher, but buy a dog that will be more amenable to this level of control.

Steady to poultry.

Close Control

I teach 'sit' and 'down' by using the word as the dog is about to sit or lie, and then praising her when she does (rather like teaching your dog to empty on command). They usually connect the two very quickly, and if you also use the hand signal with the command, then you have taught that at the same time. Equally good is the titbit method, where you hold the titbit just above the dog's line of vision to ease her into a 'sit' as she leans backwards, because otherwise she will overbalance, and bring the titbit in front of her at ground level, which will produce 'down' quite gently and naturally. There is really no need to pull dogs around but, regrettably, some trainers still do. Once your dog lies down on command, you can teach 'stay' and 'wait', remembering the difference, for a dog on 'stay' must be able to rely on you coming back, and so should remain until you do, while a dog on 'wait' must await the next command. Do not expect an untrained dog to remain indefinitely on 'stay', and always give a release command of your choice to indicate to your dog that she is now free of command and may relax 'at ease'. Examples commonly in use are 'free', 'okay' or 'go on'. I know a man who successfully unsteadies all of his dogs on the drop, because he says 'stay' with great authority and then forgets the poor dog, who, after half an hour or so, breaks its stay and wanders off. What is the command he gives it when it turns up again? 'Stay'! If you see your dog becoming restless, free her from her 'stay' before she frees herself and so weakens your authority.

After the drop close to you, start dropping her further away (use a lead, then a line, then without), until you can drop your dog at a distance. This is very useful with a working lurcher.

Absolutely vital is the recall. The nature of a lurcher's job means that she is very often out of your sight and working entirely on her own initiative, so you must be able to get her back quickly if you need to. Recall, like the drop, is taught first on a lead, then on a line, and usually goes well until the pup one day finds something – a smell, another dog, something furry to chase – that has more immediate appeal than you, and legs it. There are training books that will tell you that if you have trained your dog properly, this will not happen. Rubbish. You are not the worst dog trainer in the world, you are just a normal person with a normal puppy that has been tempted by the lure of a new experience. There is a French proverb: 'It is a bad colt that does not break his halter', so do not despair at your youngster's show of spirit. But what can you do in a situation like this?

Don't bother running after her unless she is very tiny. Even a lurcher with a broken leg can run faster than you, and if you start to run, puppy will think this is all a merry game and run even faster. You must run as fast as you can in the opposite direction. It is no good standing there yelling your dog's name, because you are simply embedding in her mind that you can yell and she doesn't have to come. But if you are running away, you are being different and interesting, and she might very well leave her new toy and come running after you instead. If she does, make her welcome. Never, ever punish a dog that has come back to you. If she runs part way back to you and then hesitates, become even more interesting – curl up on the ground, make squeaky noises, turn your back on her as if you are hiding something from her. When she comes back, do not put her straight on the lead. ('I come back – lead goes on – no more fun – I won't come back next time'), but praise her, play with her if she is a playful sort, run along a few steps with her bouncing along beside you, then on with the lead, more bouncing and squeaking so that the lead does not mean the end of fun, then after a few minutes on the lead, if you are safe from distractions, let her off again. Don't set yourself up for disobedience by letting her off the lead while there are things like rabbits about, and resign yourself to looking like the village idiot from time to time as you run away and roll on the ground squeaking. There is a lot to be said for not conducting your early training sessions in public!

A word about the use of titbits, which can be controversial. While many people may become addicted to gambling, no one ever got hooked on a vending machine. If you dispense titbits routinely, they lose their power, but if sometimes there is a titbit, the dog will be keen to see if this is one of those times.

Dealing with Disobedience

No matter how careful you are, and how good your dog is, there will be a time when she stands at a distance and defies you. This is something that needs nipping in the bud fast, for it only gets worse. This is also where old-fashioned training advice can make you want to scream with sheer frustration. You can't run faster than a running dog, and a check line is too short, whereas one that is long enough is dangerous. You need to convince the dog that you can always reach her at a distance. You may be Dead-Eye Dick with a clod of earth, in which case throw one at her. It explodes dramatically, doesn't injure the dog, and smartens her ideas up no end. If, however, like me you couldn't hit a barn door standing beside it, what you need is a catapult. Don't waste time on the traditional hazelwood and knicker elastic of your

Hand signals: lie down.

childhood, for hazelwood needs skill, and knickers aren't made that way any more. You can buy fairly cheaply a strong plastic and metal catapult with all the range and accuracy you will need, even for a rapidly departing lurcher pup. It took me two afternoons of practice following some helpful advice from an ex-serviceman who had used them in rather more interesting circumstances than dog-training, and then even I could hit my target. What do you use? Acorns or hazelnuts, either of which sting without damaging and are bio-degradable, so may be left where they fall.

Do not use your catapult with the Y arms upright, as in the 'Just William' style, as you can get a far greater range lying it on its side, with the branches of the Y to the right if you are right-handed, otherwise to the left. Assuming right-handedness, hold the stem of the catapult in your left hand with left arm fully horizontally extended. Sight between the branches of the Y and then draw the elastic and chosen missile back to your ear. Watch that acorn go!

Very few dogs need this more than once, after which they realize that you can reach them at a distance. I had a very hard-headed bitch who only had to see me take the catapult out of my pocket and she would return to heel, having had a single encounter with an acorn.

A hunting dog needs to be smart on the recall, otherwise misery follows for both of you. It is a discipline that is easily damaged in a dog that works at a distance from you, for not only must she range out to find game, she then courses it, unlike the gundog whose steadiness is reinforced every time it drops to flush or freezes on point. Therefore take the trouble to re-inforce your recall training from time to time, and avoid the competitions that are becoming fashionable where you are required to recall a dog and then halt it from the recall to give it a different com-mand. The recall should be just that, as fast as decently possible, and right back to you. If she expects to be halted before she reaches you, then you have the beginnings of unsteadiness.

Wait . . .

Retrieving

The retrieve is a subject that drives some lurcher owners to despair. Unlike gun-dogs, lurchers easily sicken of retrieving, and after one or two returns of the dummy to please you, will say clearly something to the effect of if you want the thing so much, why keep throwing it away? Some lurchers are natural retrievers, as are some purebred deerhounds, whippets and greyhounds – I have seen grey-hounds straight off the track returning rabbits live to hand without a single minute of training. Other dogs are reluctant retrievers, or refuse point-blank even to consider it. Some will fetch a caught rabbit but not a thrown dummy, while others will enjoy dummy work but stand over their quarry once they have caught it. Retrieving is a fragile skill for lurchers unless they are bred with it in mind. Some strains can make fine retrievers, as well as certain individuals with a strong gundog or Border Collie influence. All dogs can carry, for a bitch will carry food to her pups, or carry the pups to safety, and a dog will carry food to his bitch. I had a bitch who would not even consider a retrieve until she had whelped her first litter, which awakened the carrying instinct in her. The astute trainer takes advantage of unlikely opportunities like these, and this bitch became a competent retriever as long as I did not ask too much of her.

Little puppies will pick things up and carry them, and can easily be conned into carrying their treasure towards you, if you organize their bed behind you (where they want to go) and a narrow corridor in front (where there is nowhere to go) and, calling them in your sweetest voice, inter-cept them en route. Then one day it all goes to pot, for why should she give her toy to you? Unlike more ebullient breeds, running dogs seldom get excited by games of throw-and-fetch, and if you take her prize from her and throw it again, she will either see that you don't have the chance to get hold of it a second time, or she will refuse to 'fetch' it again, for, after all, what is the point? If you have a titbit sort of dog,

. . . and go!

you may be able to swap the toy for a titbit, but most lurchers won't buy that one. If she will retrieve, stop the exercise after one or two, and don't fuss about presentation. If she refuses absolutely, don't force the issue. Sometimes the loan of a cheerful old Labrador that loves retrieving will work, letting the lurcher watch the Labrador enjoying herself, and then letting the lurcher join in, for the old hand won't be put off just because there is a lurcher pup hanging off one ear. Sometimes even this won't work, but you may still have a dog that retrieves quarry straight to you, in which case there is nothing to worry about. If she is the catch-and-pin sort, you have the option of leaving it at that, for sometimes it happens in its own time that your dog will start to retrieve.

The alternative is to force-train. I detest force-training, but it does work in a percentage of cases. That means it fails in a percentage as well. It is enacted in two stages: the dog is made to hold the dummy on command by the handler tugging sharply on one ear or cheek until she opens her mouth to yelp, and then the dummy is quickly – and you do have to be quick – put in her mouth, with the hand holding up her lower jaw so that she can't spit it out. At the same time, the command 'hold' is given. The dog will soon open her mouth and take the dummy at the command. The dummy is held progressively lower and further away until the dog is stepping forward to take the dummy from the ground. When this part of the exercise has been soundly learned, the dog is led out to the dummy a few paces away, and then sent out by herself. Almost all dogs will 'hold', but some never manage to go out and pick up. There is another method that I have seen one trainer use successfully, but I consider it detrimental to the dog's well-being and so will not describe it.

Lurchers will often retrieve one particular item and nothing else. It could be a

Find a retrieve object that the pup likes.

rolled-up ball of socks stuffed with newspaper (unwashed socks, please – so much nicer to the dog), a particular dummy – most of them like a light puppy dummy – a rabbit skin, or a favourite toy. Lots of dogs detest fur in their mouths unless the pulse is still going, and will not pick up a rabbit-fur dummy, although some will tackle it if the fur is on the inside. Few will pick feather initially, but the gundog trainers' trick of wrapping the bird in a stocking, then cutting a hole and letting the wings out, will often overcome this reluctance. Lurchers tend to be faddy about cold game, but very enthusiastic about the real warm McCoy! Give your dog objects to carry when she is out with you, and if she picks something up, call her to you, take her trophy, and praise her. One of my most popular retrieve articles is a well-worn flat cap, and I do get through a few caps, but the dogs like the feel and smell of them, and seldom refuse to pick one up.

If, however, despite all your hard work, your dog has not got retrieving on her list of achievements, remember the words of an excellent dog trainer that I know, who says quite simply that it is better to have a dog that catches and doesn't retrieve than one that retrieves and doesn't catch. Lest you think that he is making a virtue of necessity, I would add that all his dogs retrieve well. Another equally perceptive trainer comments that most lurchers do not take the pleasure in retrieving that gundogs do, and will not trouble with an easy retrieve. However, some will bring you a difficult retrieve. I have one bitch who will retrieve from half a mile, or out of thick woodland, only to stop and pin the catch when she is within a few feet of me. Walking/running away or calling her in does not work. One day, she retrieved a rabbit shot by a friend, and to do so, negotiated a fence, crossed a water-filled ditch that was at the limit of her capabilities, tackled a second fence, raced across a field, picked the rabbit and returned at speed through the same obstacles to push the rabbit into my hands. A few minutes later another rabbit was shot, and she did it again. Lurchers are full of surprises.

Standing presentation; pup aged five months.

Don't place too much emphasis on retrieving. Some lurchers will do it, some won't, some might. There is nothing like live to hand for convenience, but don't despair if you have one of the many otherwise good lurchers that won't even consider it. If you are lamping your dog hard, she will have a lot more runs in her if she is not coming back the same distance with every rabbit, and have some sympathy with a dog that has done some running and has to pin her rabbit in order to get her breath back. Be careful not to sicken your dog if she will retrieve, and do not condemn her if she won't. There are far worse faults in lurchers, and I have seen a number of red-hot retrievers that can't hunt worth a light. I know which I'd be buying dog food for.

Jumping

There is disagreement over whether lurchers should be taught to jump. Some are naturals, and can scale the most awesome heights: at time of writing, the lurcher high jump record stands at 11ft 2in (3.4m). It is commonplace for a lurcher to clear a five-bar gate from a standstill with no discernible effort. It is equally common for lurchers to refuse to leave the ground at all. Unlike retrieving, jumping is a skill that can be taught to every lurcher, but do you really want to?

A lurcher that knows she can jump is the devil to confine. Lamping lurchers have been killed when leaping obstacles in the dark. There are times when it is a nuisance to have a dog that comes off her quarry when a fence or hedge intervenes, and times when it can be a relief. As so often with working dogs, there is no right or wrong answer – you must consider the

work that you want her to do, and the terrain that you want her to do it over. You will lose few rabbits with a dog that does not jump, some foxes and rather a lot of hares. If you would like your dog to jump, this is how to teach her.

Please do not, as I have read, start a tiny whelp scrambling over an obstacle to get to her food or her littermates, and then raise this obstacle higher daily. Soft bones and immature joints will be ruined, and your dog could become a cripple in early middle age. Consider the leaping action: the hindlegs may thrust together, but the dog always lands on the same front leg. The concussion from the weight of the whole dog plus gravity plus the height of the obstacle is taken by the toes, wrist and shoulder of a single leg. Therefore until your dog is a year old, or older for larger models, forget the jumping training. Some may discover the joys of jumping for themselves, so if you have one of these 'naturals', don't tell her off for jumping – that will give you problems later – but see that her opportunities for doing it are few.

Any fit dog of any age can be taught to jump quite easily. Choose your command – 'over' is usual, but I regret that mine are taught 'hup' because that is the command for horses, and I was teaching horses to jump for many years before I taught dogs. (Working Spaniels are taught 'hup' for 'sit' – you can see that this command has its drawbacks, but it works well enough for lurchers.) Your obstacle should be something like a pole on the ground. Jog up to it with your dog on the lead and hop over the pole, giving the dog her command to jump as you do so. She will bound over it with you, hardly noticing something so low. Then raise the pole a few inches, perhaps on a couple of bricks, and do the

Retrieving the real thing.

same again. That is quite enough for a first lesson.

Before you progress to bigger obstacles, you need to be sure that the landing side of the jump is not going to damage her. Going back to the horse world, it is useful to hire or borrow a sand school or similar working arena, for not only are there plenty of jumps to hand, but you may be sure that the surface is yielding and will not harm your dog. Most horse people are so amused by the thought of a dog being taught to jump that they will not charge for the use of the arena, but even if you have to pay, it should not be expensive as you will only need ten minutes at a time. Once your dog is happy with the pole on the ground, you will need a large, low obstacle such as a log or a row of oblong straw bales on their wide side. Do not use anything that will rock if the dog jumps on top of it instead of over. Lead her over these obstacles too, and then sit or lie her in front of them and call her over.

You now want your lurcher to gain height, but if you simply raise the pole higher, you risk overfacing and frightening her. To teach height, increase width, that is, introduce a second pole about a foot away from the first one. To make the width, your lurcher will have to jump higher, but she will not realize that is she doing so. Start working her loose now, with plenty of excitement and reward, to make it all fun. Arrange the jump against a fence, hedge or wall so that she is not tempted to go around it, and use jump wings if they are available to encourage her into the centre of the fence. Extend the width of the jump by one more pole and raise the rearmost pole, so that the first two are, for example, 1ft (30cm) high and the third 18in (46cm). She is now clearing some height, and the time has come to let her in on the secret. Use two poles on the ground in a V shape to funnel her into the fence and one across the foot of the jump as far out from the base as the first pole is high. For example, if the first pole is 1ft high, the base pole or 'groundline' should be 1ft out from the bottom of the jump. Do not have the back pole higher than 2ft 6in (76cm) at this point, for you are teaching technique and the really high stuff can come later. As always, don't let her sour of this game, and only jump a couple of times over each fence, never letting the lesson exceed ten minutes.

Now for some fun. There are numerous Hunter Trials and equestrian cross-country events during the autumn to spring months, and many of these courses are permanent. The jumps are big, solid and inviting, and though I don't suggest that you put your dog over every one, there will certainly be plenty that are within her scope. A small crossing of the palm with silver is usually sufficient to allow you access, though many people are generous enough to waive the fee, or if it is the day before a competition, you can join the trembling throngs of riders walking the course and let your dog pop over a few fences. My dogs have been very popular for getting right into the water jump and demonstrating how deep it is! I don't need to tell you not to forget your manners: never school your dog on a competition day, even between classes, and if the people in charge of the course have been kind to you in the matter of hiring fees, a bottle of something doesn't go amiss.

Now that your dog is bounding over obstacles on command, there is one very important thing to teach her. Barbed wire is a curse that isn't going to go away. Find a low barbed-wire fence, spread your jacket across the top strand, and call your dog to jump over the padded wire. After that, do the same with sheep fencing (not the electrified sort!). A dog that is trained to jump over your jacket can safely be put over most fences.

Keep lessons short, keep fences low, and your dog will jump with confidence. Mine have had to go over some appalling 'jumps' in obedience competitions, including a length of orange plastic netting such as

Standing presentation.

Sitting presentation.

you see around roadworks, and over a sack on a line. My dogs are not natural jumpers, but have learned to jump up to sheep-fencing height on command (though one did scale a 6ft fence to follow me after a lot of money had been spent building a dog pen at our new house). If you want your dog for working, it is quite enough for her to be able to clear about 4ft (1.2m). If she is a natural athlete and you want to compete with her, check the ground on which she is expected to land, and be wise about withdrawing her from the event if the landing side of the fence is hard, uneven or unstable (I have seen uncut bales used). No ribbon in the world is worth a crippled dog.

Stockbreaking

Stockbreaking is a very important part of your lurcher's education, for if you are working her it will be on farms and estates, forestry and commonland, which

will all be bristling with things that she should not catch. Any untrained dog will chase stock, but a lurcher is capable of catching and killing it, so a lurcher that is not stockbroken is a liability. The younger you stockbreak your lurcher the better, though it is perfectly possible to train adult dogs. I recommend that you start with sheep, as these pose the greatest temptation with the greatest possible reward to the dog, that is, an easy kill.

Sheep

There are some wonderful bar-room legends on how to sheep-break a dog. Sooner or later, someone will tell you to tie the dog in a passage and drive a flock of sheep over her, which is possibly illegal and certainly risks permanent physical and mental damage to the dog, even supposing you can muster a flock of sheep, a passage and a helpful assistant to drive them. Have you heard the one about dressing a white Bull Terrier in a sheepskin and letting your dog loose in a field with it? More feasible is the idea of confining a dog in a pen with a stroppy sheep, and letting the sheep give the dog a hiding, but again, this is possibly illegal and will not work with a high-couraged dog, which may instead develop an implacable hatred of sheep. Your dog must be indifferent to sheep, not reactive to them, and it is quite simple, albeit rather time-consuming, to achieve this.

First, she must be familiar with the words 'No' and 'Leave it'. These are the cornerstones of stockbreaking. Because there is instant reward in stock-worrying that is far superior to any reward that you can offer as an alternative, you must be prepared to use harsh actions to reinforce your command if necessary. Take her, on that lead, into the company of sheep, first outside the field that they are in. If she takes any interest in them, perhaps bouncing or tugging on the lead, tell her 'No – Leave it!' in your harshest tone, and accompany the command with a sharp jerk on the lead and a loud noise, such as the slap of a rolled-up newspaper or a length of rubber hose against the fence. Then go into the field with the pup on a check line. If the sheep run away, this creates a very strong chase stimulus in the pup, so break her eye contact by getting between her and the departing flock, and yell at her, jerk the line, slap that paper. Let the flock settle down, and walk her back and forth through them. If she tries to chase, use voice, line and noise as threateningly as you can. Some dogs will need to be gripped by the scruff and shaken, while you maintain angry eye contact and a verbal barrage, but be sensible to the fact that a frightened lurcher may bite. They have big mouths and can do a lot of damage, so a muzzle may be appropriate with a very strong-minded dog. If the sheep crowd around you, the dog is likely to be frightened with minimal additional help from you, and will

One dog waits for the other to return.

try to run away or hide behind you, but a dog that is steady in the presence of bold sheep may well be undone by the sight of them running away, so don't assume that the job is finished so easily.

Once your dog will walk through the flock without looking at the sheep, do a few down–wait–recall exercises on the line, then without the line. This job is usually complete in two sessions, and I have only ever once had to throw a dog and kneel on it to reinforce my views. One of my most difficult dogs needed only minimal sheep-breaking, but you never can tell how it is going to go until you get in there with them. I hate sheep-breaking dogs because it is necessary to be so hard on them at a time when I have done nothing but build up trust, but the enraged farmer with the 12-bore has the law behind him, and there is rarely a second chance. Nor is there any permission to be had if it gets around that one of your dogs once worried a sheep, so this is a lesson best got across early and quickly. It will also need reinforcing at intervals until the pup is two years old, by which time the lesson should be fixed in her mind.

Cattle

Cattle, and particularly bullocks, are a different case entirely. Stay right away from them if you have a dog with you, for race memory of wolves is such that cattle will attack a person with a dog, whereas they tend merely to follow and possibly surround a walker without one. Dogs have been trampled to death by herds of bullocks, and on several occasions so has the dog's owner. It is not recommended to keep the dog on a lead, for this simply reduces her chances of escape and focuses the target area on the pair of you. If the footpath crosses a field of cattle, go another way, if you see them when you are out lamping, keep out of that field, for the bright light can stampede them, and if a farmer wants you to ferret in a field of cattle, assure him that you will as soon as they are moved. Such a risk is not to be taken.

Horses

Horses are even more of a hazard than bullocks. A horse's main line of defence is running away, and when they really get going, they run blind. Generally speaking, bullocks run towards you and horses run away (except for entire males and mares with foals at foot), but the damage to legs, paddocks and fencing ends up just the same. Horses are generally worth more than cattle as well. Older horses, especially those that have been hunting, become very excited when they see dogs, and even a pleasantly excited horse is dangerous at both ends. Horses are more athletic than bovines, and can easily kill or cripple a dog with a flying kick. It won't improve your day if you get in the way either. Colts and stallions are very territorial, and take exception to strange animals and people, and mares with foals at foot can be even more aggressive. Horses have long, swinging tails which just beg a young lurcher to grab hold, making the horse leap and gallop.

I have kept horses for many years, and I am always careful about initial introductions, stockbreaking my own dogs with my own horses just as carefully as if they were stranger's. If you own both, remember the power of jealousy, for a horse that seems to have accepted a dog may just be biding its time. However friendly a horse and dog arrangement

A good jump for training.

seems to be, never trust it, for large herbivores are unpredictable. Nor should you expect a special friendship to extend to others of that species: individuals of different species can form strong friendships, but it is strictly a matter between those two individuals, and would not extend to a strange horse or dog. Conversely, a horse or cow that hates dogs will probably hate all dogs. The good news is that horses, unlike cattle, tend to mind their own business, and so do not charge up to harass a dog in the way that bovines will. As long as they have not been frightened by dogs, they will merely favour you with a glance before they get back to the serious business of eating, therefore as long as your dog has been steadied to horses, you can cross the field by the footpath. Never lamp a horse field, however, and I personally do not ferret them either, unless the horses have been removed first. Lovely creatures though they be, they are better somewhere different from where your dog is chasing a rabbit.

Cats

Cats present a lot of difficulties. All dogs instinctively want to chase cats, but a longdog is capable of catching and killing them, and you absolutely do not want this to happen. The cat is somebody's beloved pet, and it is also capable of blinding your dog. It is easy enough to start a lurcher off on friendly terms with cats, especially if you have cats of your own, but the cat side of the arrangement is untrustworthy in that a cat will court a friendly dog, purr and rub up against it with every sign of amiability, and then turn and lacerate the dog's face with its claws. The most cat-friendly of lurchers can be turned into a cat-hating fiend after one or two doses of this, so if possible, I break things up at the purr-and-rub stage, unless I know that the cat is an honest one. A lurcher that is safe with family cats and others that she knows will still chase a cat that erupts out of nowhere and pelts past her, and though the lurcher may not intend the cat any harm, the cat does not know this. Lurchers that play nicely with cats, as mine do, will also try to play with a strange cat that does not know the rules, which can lead to a frightened cat and an extremely acid cat owner. People who allow their cats to stray can still get remarkably offended if said cat is then chased by a dog, and though the cat has no status in law and therefore no crime has been committed, the cat is still someone's pet. A blinded dog or a devastated cat owner are situations that must be avoided if at all possible.

Water

There are some areas of dog training that are pure pleasure, and introducing your dog to water is one of them. Longdogs love water, and you will be pleasantly surprised to see the dog that minces around puddles on the tips of her toes surge into deep water with an expression of utter

bliss, speedboating along in a series of leaps. There are several very good reasons for wanting your dog to be confident and happy about going into water.

Running dogs overheat easily, and can die if they over-exert themselves on a hot day. You cannot be certain that something will not pop out of covert on the most unsuitable of days, and if your dog comes back staggering, eyes glazed, corners of mouth turned back, and gasping with a harsh, fluttering breathing that is once heard never forgotten, she needs help fast. If there is water, get her into it and pour it over her. If she can enter water of her own volition, she will lie down in it until she feels better; if there is no water, mud will cool her almost as well. I have lifted dogs into cattle troughs before now, and if you cannot avoid walking your dog in the hot part of the day rather than the relative cool of the early morning and evening, carry water in the car and choose routes that are punctuated by streams and water

Log over ditch.

troughs. A dog that will readily enter water on command is a safer dog than one that is frightened to. Another reason for wanting your dog to be amphibious is so that she will if necessary be able to pick quarry out of water. Rabbits and hares will swim if they have to, and if you shoot over your lurcher, it is useful for her to be able to retrieve out of water. Dogs that are reluctant retrievers on land will often retrieve enthusiastically out of water, and though I have no idea why this should be, I have used it successfully to encourage a non-retriever to retrieve.

However, lurchers are not Spaniels, and do not have the urge to throw themselves into water – any water – that is apparent in many breeds of gundog. The first introduction to water should therefore be as gentle and pleasurable as possible, so you need a warm day, a quiet stretch of shallow water with a firm bottom to it, and an easy access with a gently sloping bank. An additional dog that is already a keen water-hound is invaluable, but if it is just you and your pup, you will still manage easily. This is one occasion where you do not have your dog on a lead, because she must enter the water of her own will and in her own time.

Go to the edge of the water and let her watch. Perhaps she will come to the edge with you, perhaps she will drink. Speak to her in encouraging tones if she does. Then you go into the water a little way; she may follow you, she may not. Praise her if she comes in, but ignore her if she does not, and wade out a little further. Presently, one leg will go in, then another, then she will stand and think. She may back out and then go in again, or she may plant herself on the bank and look sad as you wade out further. Come out of the stream and play a game with her until she is thoroughly hot, then walk back into the water, not looking back at her. It may take one session, it may take several, but she will eventually go into the water and enjoy it. Never lift or drag her in, don't splash her or pile on the pressure by throwing a favourite toy into the water, just leave it as a perfectly unremarkable situation, and she will follow at her own pace, just as she follows you everywhere else. Keep the experience pleasant: don't take her in out of her depth, or get so far away from her that she panics, backs out and runs along the bank. In my experience, if you choose the right area of water and allow the dog plenty of time, you will have no trouble at all in getting her to like water, though you may experience

---

The Benefits of Water

The other main reason for encouraging your dog to like water is that wading is an excellent physical therapy. A running dog that is returning to fitness after injury can exercise herself more safely in water than on land, because she will be going slowly and steadily, pushing against the bulk of water. If she has been restricted to lead exercise, water is a good way of giving her more work without the risk of her dashing about and stressing the newly healed injury. Racehorse trainers know all about the benefits of walking their fragile and highly-strung charges in water. Wading tightens tendons and builds muscle, but does not harden feet, so should be used in conjunction with steady road walking.

Over a stile.

considerable trouble in getting her to come out again once she finds out how nice it all is!

It is rare for running dogs to find sufficient depth of water in which to swim, and with their long legs and narrow bodies, they do not find it as easy as a chunky, short-legged Spaniel or Labrador would, so do not worry about swimming them unless you have an absolutely safe area of water available. Don't forget that a swimming dog will still try to follow you 'to heel' which can result in you getting a badly scratched back, as she doesn't realize that you walk vertically but swim horizontally, and can therefore rake you with her front paws. I stick to wading exercise, making sure that there is nothing nasty on the bed of the brook, for people have a depressing habit of throwing rubbish into water. If your regular walks take in areas where your dog can enter water and play safely, she will have learned something useful as well as gained a little extra fitness.

Changing Direction

A dog that will turn on command can be directed precisely onto quarry. Often there is a situation when the human can see a sitting rabbit or hare that the dog cannot, or you may wish to lieu your dog in on scent where you have just seen a fox get up. The conventional whistle signal for this is two pips, accompanied by an extravagant sweeping movement of the arm in the direction that the handler wants the dog to take. Some gundog handlers use a white handkerchief in the hand so that the dog can see better where she is supposed to go. Use whatever voice, whistle or signals you prefer, as long as you are consistent.

Turning to command is easy to teach, and you start with that little puppy that follows you everywhere. When she has stopped to examine a smell, you change the direction in which you are walking, and when her head goes up to look for you, give your command and she will change direction quite naturally. Some trainers fling a titbit for the dog to find, though I have never needed to with mine. If your dog likes finding dummies or searching out dead rabbits, plant some for her to find and retrieve when you signal her on to them. When you progress to allowing her to chase rabbits, go out in the set-aside where you have a good view of them, especially the inexperienced little squeakers, and guide her to them. By the time that your dog starts to catch, she will be so convinced of your wisdom that she will change direction from half a mile away, as long as she can see or hear you. Combining a visual and audible signal is useful, for those windy days when sound is distorted or for when visibility is poor.

Opening Up and Hard Mouth

Two major faults in the working lurcher are 'opening up' – barking or yelping when

running on quarry – and 'hard mouth'. Both of these are incurable, so it is a good idea to explore the causes, so as to avoid them if possible. However, neither fault need be the end of the world in a dog which is otherwise a good performer, so I will also discuss ways of living with one or other situation.

Opening Up

Opening up is caused by frustration, when the dog cannot cope with its quarry either due to being worked too young or badly entered. The tendency can be inherited, which is one of the reasons that, in a terrier lurcher, the silent Bedlington is favoured over breeds of terrier that are just as efficient but have been essentially bred to be noisy (an earth dog that worked silently underground was useless in the days before locator collars and can be difficult even now). Of purebred sighthounds, the Whippet makes the most noise, though

Over barbed wire.

19in (48cm) Bedlington / Whippet tackles a 4ft (1.2m) fence.

I have not heard of many problems with Whippet crosses and I rate them highly. Of other working dogs, Border Collies can be noisy, and Bearded Collies, New Zealand Huntaways and Australian Kelpies (the Cattle Dogs less so) have to bark as part of their job, facing down and driving some very independent livestock. That is not to say that any of these crosses will definitely open up, but that 50 per cent of the genes come from dogs bred to bark, so if you press the wrong buttons, it is more likely that noise will result than from naturally silent dogs such as Salukis and Deerhounds.

The dog will open up if it is outclassed by its quarry. This can vary from the despairing 'yip' as the quarry pulls away, to a series of barks often seen when a dog comes level with a fox, but lacks the bottle to tackle it. It is very common for a running dog to give mouth in woodland, where she cannot run at full speed, nor keep her quarry in view because of the

trees. This is the start: soon the dog will start to shout at her quarry as soon as it starts to run. This volley of noise can sometimes faze a rabbit into making a mistake, which is why terriers give mouth so valiantly, but with a running dog it tells the world that this dog has been entered too soon, too unfit, or has been put onto quarry that fights back without adequate preparation. Once the habit is established, it is virtually impossible to eradicate.

Nevertheless, opening up does not stop your dog from catching quarry, and in some circumstances can prove little more than inconvenient. Whereas a lamping dog that gives mouth will put everything in earshot to ground, and a coursing dog will waste too much breath in shouting to come to terms with its quarry – thereby ensuring the continuation of the very circumstance that started all this – a ferreting dog will still mark and pin rabbits in the nets, and may even still catch the odd escapee. A rabbit bolted by a ferret will not run anything like as fast as a rabbit spotlighted in the lamp, nor as far either, and the dog may well not come under sufficient pressure to warrant her barking. On the other hand, a bushing dog that opens up is a positive advantage, as those who run mixed packs will know. The quarry tends to be bolted by terriers or small hounds, both of which are encouraged to give mouth so that the rest of us know what is going on in covert. One well-known lady hunter deliberately teaches her lurchers to open up, because she hunts out such large areas of dense undergrowth that it is essential all her dogs give mouth, so that everyone knows what is going on where.

Hard Mouth

The other fault, hard mouth, is an interesting one. It can be inherited, or it can crop up in a dog that has come from generations of soft-mouthed lurchers.

Some pundits reckon it almost a hanging crime, but in fact it is rarely more than a nuisance, and sometimes not even that. A dog can turn hard-mouthed quite suddenly, and it is not difficult to see why. When caught, some rabbits give up and hang limply in the dog's mouth, whereas some kick viciously and will deliver a bite worse than a rat's if they can. The inside of a working dog's lips will be scored with rabbit kicks, and there comes a time when a dog has simply had enough of having her face raked to the eyes by three pounds of furiously fighting rabbit. Small lurchers especially have a bad time. It makes good dog sense to bite the rabbit and kill it, carrying back a non-kicking body, and I for one cannot blame her. It should be remembered that poachers of the old days insisted on a lurcher with a 'killing mouth' so that they were not given away by the noise of a rabbit or hare squealing. Tales abound of these old-style lurchers that would kill rabbits and cache them under a hedge, to retrieve them when the coast

In full flight.

was clear. Live to hand meant a trip to the Colonies in those days!

Some dogs lose their tempers completely with a fighting rabbit and crunch it to shrapnel; some progress to doing this to every rabbit, on a 'get it before it gets me' principle, whereas some only bite rabbits that need to be silenced. One of my dogs would always kill a squealing rabbit, but bring others back alive, leading me to assume that a squealer would also be a kicker. She also tended to hold rabbits round the body, where they could kick her with more effect, whereas her mother, who never killed a single rabbit, would hold hers by the loose skin on the back, meaning they could kick as much as they liked without touching her. However, this latter dog would always kill hares as soon as she brought them down – the loose skin trick obviously did not work with such a big, long-legged animal.

It is the dog which is worked hard that is more likely to become hard-mouthed, because she encounters a higher percentage of struggling rabbits, and is also much more tired at the end of a long hunting session than a dog that only goes out for an hour or two now and then. Even so, many lurchers live long working lives without marking a single rabbit. The dog that kills with one bite will still leave a usable carcase in that the bruise is generally confined to the fore half; I know one dog that crushes the rabbit's head every time, leaving a perfectly saleable carcase. With the shoulder cruncher, the better part of the carcase, the meaty back and hindquarters, is left clean, and the fore-parts can go as ferret food, but if your dog crunches the whole carcase just enjoy your sport and feed your ferrets well, resigning yourself to being unable to sell any rabbits. The rabbits are just as dead, which will please your landowner, and you and your dog have still had a lot of pleasure out of hunting together. The market for wild rabbit is variable at best: I have had years

Praise is very important.

of being literally unable to give them away, but at the time of writing have a butcher who will take all my surplus. Another friend sells his rabbits whole to snake and hawk owners, so there are still outlets for the marked rabbits, if you have any left over from feeding your own stock.

Some dogs mark their rabbits because they strike with such determination that they bruise or even puncture the flesh, though the rabbit is brought back alive and would certainly survive if you were to let it go. The dog that is so determined to catch her quarry that she hits it hard enough to mark it is hardly displaying a fault. Each dog is different, each dog catches differently, and it is good to go out and watch other lurchers work, to see how they catch. I know a huge dog that trips his rabbits with his front feet because he does not find it easy to swoop down to their height. Then there is the exceptionally fast dog that loses his rabbits if they turn due to the fact that he is going so fast, although seldom do they

get the chance because he comes at them out of nowhere and just scoops them up. Dogs can pick up rabbits by the rump or a back leg, or they can somersault with their rabbits: every dog has her own favoured technique. A soft-mouthed dog is a treasure, but a hard-mouthed dog is really not the problem that some would have you believe.

The Shock Collar

No chapter on training is complete without a look at that controversial aid, the electric collar. At the moment, it is still legal in this country. The collar has a box on it with two probes that touch the dog's throat, allowing the handler to transmit an electric shock of varying intensity to the dog. Some collars emit a warning noise before they shock, which gives the dog one last opportunity to obey.

Having had no personal experience of these, I spent some time with a profes-

Some dogs need more than others.

Rabbits caught by a hard-mouthed dog.

sional dog behaviourist and trainer. He sees the device very much as a last resort, but correctly used, a great deal more humane than a thrashing. The collar is used only for chasing situations, such as cars or sheep, where the dog's life is in jeopardy. The collar is used in a certain sequence of events, under tightly controlled conditions, and in connection with a specific command issued to the dog by its owner – the collar is handled by the professional. When the dog disobeys its owner's command, it receives an instant reprimand in the form of a short shock – thus the dog is trained not to disobey the command, and the owner is trained in handling the dog. During the retraining period, owner and dog are set a series of exercises designed to reinforce a proper dog/owner relationship, and to strengthen the habit of obedience through kindness and firmness. After the retraining is complete, the owner must do everything possible to ensure that the dog is never subjected to the stimuli that previously resulted in the chase, and the dog must never be allowed out unsupervised, as there would be no one to issue the command that the dog has been trained to obey.

For something as sensitive as a lurcher, the collar is indeed a risky device, and for any dog it is a dreadful thing in the wrong hands – but then, so is a choke chain. The collar should only be considered in the kind of circumstance that is life-threatening for the dog, and only be used by someone who is not going to lose their temper. The electric collar is an emotive subject: in the right hands, it has saved dogs that would have otherwise died; in the wrong hands, anything is cruel. I suggest that, if you and your dog have a problem so grave that you think only the collar can help, hire an experienced professional along with it, and he or she will be able to help you with the whole of the problem, instead of just a part of it.

Continuation Training

As you and your lurcher meld into an experienced working team, you will find that you use all sorts of signals, commands, whistles and soft noises as you work with her. The downside is that sometimes you will join forces with someone who uses the same commands in a different context; for instance, the noise I use to send mine into quarry is the same one that a friend uses to bring his dog back to heel. This means that we cannot work our dogs together. Organizers of Field Trials for lurchers would do well to bear this in mind, as it is becoming popular to work two or more dogs together during the judging. This is not a good idea in my opinion, as dogs will work differently together, sometimes very differently, from how they will when solo, due to natural hierarchy and equally natural jealousy. How much more complicated is it when two well-trained dogs are getting conflicting signals?

But how good it is when it works! Recently, I was working my youngster in some tall set-aside. I prefer my dogs to work with minimum interference, so it is my habit to cast them off (command, hand signal) and allow them to quarter according to their own preference, for their understanding of scent and wind direction is far superior to mine. He was working eagerly when I saw a sitting rabbit far from covert. One whistle for 'quarry here' and a raised arm caught his attention. He came over fast, but concentrating on me as I whistled 'sitter' and swept my arm across in its direction. As he was nearly on it and casting for scent, I changed the whistle for 'close', the rabbit broke, and he was onto it. No, he didn't catch that one, but he had crossed a good thirty acres and been guided to within a snap of his rabbit, entirely on trust. And most lurchers can be trained to do that.

CHAPTER 3

ENTERING TO QUARRY

Running dogs must not be entered to quarry until they are physically and mentally ready, the timing of which is different for different crosses. A rule of thumb is to devote the first year to obedience training, and enter the dog to rabbit at the beginning of the following year, work her lightly until she is two, and thereafter all you want. This is no new idea: in Juliana Berners' *Ye Boke of St. Albans*, written in the late 1400s, she says,

> Ye first year ye shall him feed,
> Ye secon year to field him lead.

and this was written in far harder times, for her advice goes on to the dog's ninth year, when she recommends, 'have him to the tanner'. You will always hear of people entering their dogs to quarry much earlier, but it is to the detriment of the dog, and although a yearling is capable of hard work, she won't last long if that is what you let her do.

The first two years of the dog's life will see her at her fastest; thereafter, she will start to lose her speed, but develop 'quarry sense' in its stead, which will fill the game bag as well as, and possibly better than, sheer speed. Sadly, many young dogs are ruined by people seeking to capitalize on this speed, and then discarding the dog when she proves 'no good', when in fact she would probably have been plenty good enough if only she had been allowed to mature before being tested in the field. This is the main reason for the large number of sapling lurchers advertised for sale. If she is used too young, the physical damage is irreparable. Lungs, heart and kidneys are strained beyond healing, joints and bones malform, and too much muscle on a juvenile frame will deform her and prepare the ground for early arthritis and degeneration. Mental damage is as bad: the dog may become a quitter, or develop hard mouth, or the habit of opening up on quarry. If, however, you let your lurcher mature in her own time, she will remain in good health and working fettle for many years. It is worth the wait.

I have had people say to me 'but what of the wild dog?', for of course the wild dog would have to hunt its own food long before it reaches its first birthday. In fact, pack-hunting wild dogs contribute very little to the kill when they are saplings. Solitary hunters like the fox mature much faster than domestic dogs, and have a variety of undemanding food sources, such as insects, mice or nests of baby rabbits. The wild canid catches one dinner, but you are asking your lurcher to catch rabbit after rabbit. Lamping is tremendously hard on a dog, second only to coursing in the amount of effort involved, and far too much for an immature dog. There is plenty that you can do with your lurcher prior to serious hunting, so enjoy her puppyhood with her, for it goes soon enough.

Having said that, game will pop up in the unlikeliest places when you don't want to see it, and I currently possess a bitch that caught a rat when she was fourteen weeks old (it nearly sliced her nose off, for her baby teeth and jaws were barely strong enough to kill it) and her first rabbit at seven months. Her litter brother and

Steady and alert.

sister together tackled and killed a dog fox at seven months; however, another litter brother went into his first fox at ten months, got bitten, and never tackled another. No matter how careful you are, incidents like these will sometimes happen and send your training schedule spinning, but there is the world of difference between an accidental find, and the deliberate working of an immature dog.

Rabbits

Rabbits are not easy quarry for the beginner, and clumsy entering can turn a potentially good rabbit dog into an indifferent one. A dog gets frustrated when, try as she may, rabbits outrun or out-turn her, or vanish down holes just as she is getting on terms with them. Too much of this can make a dog yap as she courses, and behold! you have created a problem that cannot be solved. Or she can 'jack', that is, quit and stop chasing rabbits

altogether. In terms of physical stress, a ferreted rabbit is easier to catch then a lamped one, and healthy daytime rabbits are the hardest of all, but ferreting requires a great deal of mental concentration, and not all dogs are mature enough for that when they are starting. Except for one occasion, I have always started my lurchers off with lamping, restricting them to three or four runs at a session. The exception was a dog that I was finding a real problem to train; the long-distance world of the moonless night was out of the question with such an animal, and so I took her ferreting. She rapidly learned the ropes, though initially I had to tie her up while I netted the bury, or she would disappear off hunting on her own. The difficulty came when I started lamping her, and she expected me to whip out a ferret every time she lost a rabbit to ground, marking the bury instead of returning to hand. This was overcome with time and practice, but thereafter I reverted to teaching lamping before

---

First Quarry

The best quarry I have ever started a young dog on is mice. At the time, I had access to unoccupied farm buildings which were filled with paper feed sacks and absolutely alive with mice. Tuck trousers into socks, switch on the light, and pick up a large stick with which to lift the sacks. Shut dog and self into stable, block off mouse-sized escape routes, and gingerly lift sacks with stick. Mice whizz out like bumble bees, the dog learns to be quick on its feet and to co-ordinate eyes and mouth, and the mice die instantly. A far better death in this case than subsequently, when the landowner, putting the buildings

up for sale, had poison put down for the mice. The dogs learned to work with me, and found that if they obeyed me, there was reward in the form of an easy catch. Their confidence blossomed, and when the time came to introduce them to rabbits they were already halfway there, knowing that they could catch and that I was there to help them. I have never been so lucky since that farm was sold. If you do have access to mousing, make sure that no one is poisoning the mice, as the dog may well swallow a few before she gets going properly. Do not start your dog on rats – they come later.

ferreting, lamping being easier mentally on the dog.

When you start rabbit work, you want your dog to have some easy catches to build up her confidence. Naturally, sleek, super-fit decathlete rabbits will dominate your outings, as you desperately seek old, infirm (or very young and stupid) quarry, and this is probably the only time that I have found myxomatosis useful, in that rabbits afflicted with 'myxy' need to have a merciful end to their lives, and provide an easy catch for your dog. I have heard tell that dogs will not take on a myxy rabbit, but I have not come across this. Although the disease does not cross species as far as we know, I do not feed diseased rabbits to my stock, but leave them for the foxes. Some of these poor rabbits really do run, and many a time I have been surprised to find advanced myxomatosis in a rabbit that has given a dog a testing course. Still, they are easier to catch than a healthy rabbit, and most dogs start off this way.

You may well hear claims of huge hauls of rabbits caught by a lurcher on her first outing, but in truth you should prepare yourself for a long wait before she gets fur in her mouth. Some dogs have their feet and mouths well organized right from the beginning, while others take an age to learn their trade. One of the best catch dogs I have ever seen did not connect with a rabbit until she was past two years old and the despair of her owner. Think what your dog has to do: she has to run like hell, turn with her rabbit, cope with the dramatic change in balance as she drops her head to strike, then pick up her rabbit and bring it back to you. If she has had a hard run, she may have to put her rabbit down in order to get her breath, and may then have the frustration of seeing it run

off. Or if she is a smallish lurcher, she may find three pounds of kicking rabbit too much to cope with, and put in a killing bite before she brings it back. Annoying though this is, you can see her point, and it isn't a case of hard mouth – I've seen rabbits caught by hard-mouthed dogs that were barely fit for ferret food – so if your dog starts to do this, just make the best of it. The dog that puts her rabbit down will soon learn to pin it, and as she becomes more experienced, she will manage better.

I like my dogs to gain some experience as a roughshooter's companion, although it certainly is not a vital part of lurcher education. I do not shoot, so am free to concentrate on handling the dog, who gets a few retrieves, but most importantly learns to hunt up game in controlled circumstances. A dog needs to find game before she can catch it, and there are many lurchers who would make good Spaniels; they can and will learn to use their noses to find what is there. Initially, I did the whole thing backwards, because I had a dog that would point and flush game, and it was convenient to take her out as part of the roughshooting team. As she became older and I had to retire her, she was still able to enjoy her outings with the gun, and indeed is still a very useful contributor to the day's tally, because if game is there, she will find it. However, the gundog business should not be overdone, because you do not want your dog to drop to flush, you want her on her marks ready to go when something bolts. This means that the person with the gun must be totally reliable, for the dog will be coursing game that comes her way and it must not be shot off the end of her nose. With a lurcher or lurchers on the team, the gun is backstop, there to arrest the progress of anything that the lurchers are not on hand to chase.

Rabbit about to bolt from cover.

A lurcher must launch as soon as quarry breaks cover, and must be in no doubt that it is all right for her to do so. Also, beware of making her gun-shy. It is exceptionally easy with such sensitive dogs; I have had one go gun-shy, and it took eleven months to get her right again. Start off with the .22 and the .410 before the 20- and 12-bore, introducing the louder bangs from a distance. My once gun-shy dog now runs towards the shot because it means a 'catch', and she who is an indifferent retriever has done some smart and flawless retrieves to the gun.

Lamping

When you are ready to start your lurcher on the lamp, take her out with it at night and let her see rabbits in the beam. At first, she will look everywhere except where she is supposed to, for her night vision is far better than yours, but be patient and she will start to follow the beam. Rabbits will get up and run: do not slip her, but follow the running rabbit with the spotlight. Do not use your best lamping ground for this! Rather choose an area where the rabbits are already lamp-shy, so that you do not ruin a good piece of ground, but the dog has plenty of movement to look at. Only let her watch a very few rabbits, so that she does not start to yip with frustration at not being allowed to chase. Next time out, let her watch a made dog lamping, but again, only a couple of runs, for if she is made of the right stuff, she will start to wriggle and squeak on the slip, and you need a steady, silent dog for this discipline. If the rabbits are obliging, let her have one run. You need a rabbit that is far from cover, so choose it carefully and do not expect her to catch it. If she does, make a fuss of her and take her home. If she does not, still make a fuss of her, let her watch a couple more, and if you find a likely one, give her one more run. Whatever the result, go home after that. It is terribly tempting to go on and on in the hope of a catch, but few dogs can cope with continual failure, and it doesn't do to underestimate what hard work lamping is for your dog. No matter how fit she is – and make sure she is fit before you start to work her – the twisting and turning, uneven going and the excitement will take a lot out of her, physically and mentally.

Far more important at this stage than any number of rabbits in the bag is to have your dog coming straight back to you after every run. She must obey – lamp off = come back; you do not want her hunting on in the dark. Lots of them do to start with, and if yours does, grit your teeth and walk away, back to your car. She will follow you, though she may take her time. Suppress your anger and disappointment, for she will sense them, and may not come to hand. When she finally does, just greet her in a friendly, matter-of-fact manner, and wait for twenty minutes or so before you start again. She will soon learn that the best fun follows when she comes to hand. Don't ever, while you are training her, put the lamp on another rabbit while she is still out there having lost the first one. Nothing encourages freelancing more. You will need the patience of several saints at this time, but if patience is not one of your many virtues, you would be better off with a less sensitive stamp of canine companion.

Suppose you do not have a made dog available to lamp your dog with? No problem, it will just take a few nights longer. Choose a well-placed rabbit for her, get her as close as you can before it runs, and urge her onto it. What do I mean by a well-placed rabbit? It should be a long way from cover, and you should walk over to it. A rabbit that runs head-on at a dog is very

difficult to stop; a rabbit running away may be followed well, and a rabbit that crosses broadside may be intercepted most easily. Be absolutely sure that your lurcher is sighted, for she is a lot shorter than you and cannot see as far. A dog that is anxious to hunt may buck and leap at the end of the slip, thereby convincing you that she has seen the rabbit, but when you launch her you find that she has not. Too many incidents like this will weaken your trust in each other, so take your time and be certain that she has seen the rabbit you want her to chase. Even so, she may not chase to start with, or she may run a few yards then scuttle back to you. If this happens, call her right in and praise her, for coming back to hand is the most valuable lesson, and the rest will fall into place later.

Suppose you have a canine wonder that catches her first rabbit on the lamp spot-on? Now here is a delicate situation. If she comes back to hand, rabbit and all, you've done a good job, she is the right stuff, and you want it to stay that way. Your degree of reaction will depend on the character of your dog. If she is an excitable sort, be casual, praise her briefly, take the rabbit quietly and despatch it. On the other hand, if your dog is a shy sort, praise her lavishly and assure her that she is the best dog ever as you take her rabbit. She will be very pleased with her first rabbit, and may want to mouth it or dance round you wagging her tail. Be gentle with her, let her sniff her rabbit but discourage any attempt at mouthing with 'no – dead', and when the mood has settled, go home. The first lurcher I ever trained was very subdued after her first rabbit, riding home in silence in the car. She carried the rabbit soberly into the cottage, let me take it from her, and seemed ready to settle for the night when the excitement suddenly hit her, and she ran squealing round the cottage, upstairs, downstairs, on and off the furniture in an ecstatic wall-of-death display that culminated in her stealing one of my socks and hiding it. I never found out where, but then I am better at dog training than housework.

I know that there are people who like to ride their luck and continue lamping, but this first time it is better to wrap up the lesson there and then, building on it next time out.

When It Goes Wrong

What if it all goes pear-shaped? There are a lot of alternatives that you won't read about in most of the training manuals. Your dog may retrieve to you and then hang on grimly to the rabbit. Do not attempt to wrench if from her and on no account start a tug-of-war (never play this game with a working dog of any sort), but take hold of as much rabbit as you can with one hand and soothe your dog with the other, talking softly to her until she relaxes her grip. If you make her sit, it will all happen fairly gracefully. You may be able to persuade her to accept a titbit in lieu of the rabbit, but relatively few lurchers will respond to offers of food when they have their very first warm fuzzy rabbit in their mouths. But she won't hold on to it for ever, so speak quietly to her until she relaxes, and when she does, take the rabbit gently, do not snatch it. Your patience with this first rabbit will save you a lot of grief later, for do you really think she will retrieve another rabbit for you if you bully her into parting with her trophy? After you have taken and despatched the rabbit, let her sniff it but not take it back, and tell her how clever she is.

You may have a dog that has absolutely no intention of letting you have her rabbit. She may gallop around you with the rabbit in her mouth, or tear off across the field to find somewhere private to eat it. She may kill it and drop it and come

A neat pick-up.

back without it. None of this means that you are a lousy trainer, or that she is a useless dog; believe me, you will get where you are going but it will take a little longer. Stop and think – why should she let you have her rabbit? It is not necessarily a dominance display, for some very submissive dogs will run off with their rabbit, but be patient, for if you lose your temper with this particular type of dog you will never get her right.

It is the novelty factor. As she becomes more blasé about her rabbits, she will become easier to handle. She needs work and more work. I had one of these dogs, and I took her on holiday to Scotland with me, to an area on the north coast that was absolutely infested with rabbits. I ferreted and bushed with her all day, and lamped her for half the night for five days and nights. I bottomed her and I nearly bottomed myself as well, but it cured her. This was a drastic remedy for an outstandingly difficult dog, and most won't need anything like so dramatic a cure. For the immediate problem, what you must not do is allow her respite to eat the rabbit. Forget all the training books that tell you never to go to your dog but make her come to you – if she eats that rabbit, your lamping is finished for the night, and she has well and truly bested you. Walk – don't run – after her, never allowing her time to stop, but neither making her panic and run. Stop when she stops, move if she tries to eat, stalk her, but sweetly, so that she knows she may come to you if she wishes. If you are very calm about the whole thing, eventually you will be able to get a hand on the rabbit. Just hold it there, don't snatch it from her, then gently put her on the slip and lead her away, taking up the rabbit as you go. Thus you have mastered her, infinitely quietly, and reaffirmed the fact that you are in charge of the night's proceedings. Then quit while you are ahead and go home. Next day, go through the obedience routine for ten minutes or so, and if you take her lamping the following night, precede the hunting with a few minutes of obedience, to reinforce the habit. One thing you must not do is give her the 'down' command and then walk up to her and take her rabbit, because she won't fall for that one again, which will then undermine your authority, not to mention her 'down–stay'.

If the dog circles you but will not come in – a common problem if there is another dog about – it is easier to deal with, because in fact she would like to come in, but is not completely certain that she should. If you have started her with another dog, that dog should have a different handler and be kept well clear of you when your dog starts to return. Otherwise, until your dog is fully trained, she is best lamped solo. If you are on your own and she is circling, there are a number of ways you can win. If walking or running away does not encourage her to follow, shine the lamp past you and then switch it off as she comes to the beam, making a big fuss of her as you apprehend her. Whatever you do, don't speak harshly to her, much as you would like to, because that gives her no incentive to return. A dog that circles or runs off is suffering a conflict of loyalties, but she's only a dog and a young one at that, so you will have to be the one to display emotional maturity. Your dog can run faster than you, so there is never any point in chasing her. But if you walk after her, talking in a firm and kindly voice, you will eventually be able to enter into negotiations about the possession of the rabbit. This is only one rabbit, remember, and neither here nor

A killing mouth.

there in view of the rabbits you and your dog will catch together in the future.

Take the time to get things right in the beginning. Foul up on the early exercises, and you will be given proof that lurchers cannot be treated like more robust-natured dogs such as Labradors. Lurchers don't forget and they may not forgive; bad as it may look to you now, believe me, it can get an awful lot worse. You must always be straight with your lurcher. Don't take any nonsense, but never be dishonest with her. You are both on the same side in that you both want that rabbit; you just have to get it through to her that there is more fun doing it your way than hers. Don't make an issue of that rabbit, but once you have hold of most of it, and she is thinking about slackening her grip, make a fuss of her, and let her give it up in her own time. Don't snatch it away when she does, but continue to praise her, letting her sniff the rabbit but not mouth it. Then put her in a down–stay, walk away and then call her to you. Once again, you have

established the habit of obedience. Then put her on the slip, give her the rabbit to carry, and walk smartly along until she is settled in trotting beside you carrying the rabbit. Presently, you can make her sit, and take the rabbit again, this time to put it in your pocket or gamebag.

As you see, early lamping nights may be quite a headache, or they may go like clockwork. What I have found from working with a great many dogs is that obedience training doesn't matter a jot when things go well, but is worth gold when they go wrong. I know lurchers that have retrieved live to hand from day one without any training – it has all been instinctive and inborn. If you are lucky enough to have such a dog, be grateful, but don't be deluded into thinking that she is so good because you haven't trained her, or that training is a waste of time. One day, you may own a right little madam, and that is when the obedience training pays off, because you will be able to change her around and make a good lurcher out of her, where a lesser person would simply 'out' her as being no good. Most lurchers are very amiable about handing over their catch, but if you have one of the other sort, be prepared to work at it. Go home and re-establish your obedience training – don't overdo it, just run through the basics together. Take her for a good long walk before you next go lamping, so that she is tired, for a tired dog will be less likely to boil over with excitement when she catches. Also, check how you are feeding her, which is covered in detail in Chapter Six on Care and Maintenance. Some very good working dogs have been right little minxes when they started, so keep faith with her.

On the opposite end of the scale is the dog that will not run. Dogs with 50 per cent or more Border Collie blood are especially prone to this, having a tendency to stalk which often pays off in daylight but is not at all the idea on the lamp, unless you work an area where the rabbits tend to sit tightly. This is one of the few occasions when I would suggest running her with another dog, but only on a few occasions. Let her watch the other dog lamping, then let her have a go on her own; if she starts to stalk, slip the other dog. If you don't have the use of another dog, stop lamping her for a few weeks and concentrate on daylight work. Experiment with her weight (*see* Care and Maintenance) and feed. She will become a lamping dog in time.

Style

Different dogs have very different lamping styles. None is good or bad, as long as the end result is a rabbit. I have seen dogs that go straight down the beam, dogs that dodge out of the light and come into the running rabbit from the darkness, dogs that work the rabbit away from its desti-nation like a goalkeeper, dogs that use blistering speed to overwhelm a rabbit without taking a single turn out of it. Some dogs strike like snakes, some take with

Marking an unnetted hole.

such conviction that they somersault, others trip the rabbit up with their front paws and then pick it up. A dog must work within her own physical limitations, and you and she must evolve a lamping style that suits her abilities. You can't make a slow dog a fast one, and a big dog will never out-turn a little one, but all of them will catch if you choose the right rabbit. Some dogs will not face cover, others would face Satan himself, but you won't make a hedge-splitter out of a cover-shy dog, so don't put her in that position. You have to play the hand that you are dealt, so make the most of her talents. As your dog becomes more experienced, she will learn to slow up as she reaches her rabbit, expecting it to turn, and it is often on the turn that the rabbit is picked up. To begin with, the rabbit will turn and the dog will carry on, which is why rabbits do it, but the dog will learn. This is why many made hunting dogs make lousy lure-chasing or racing dogs, because they will slow down as they reach the lure – that's if they bother to chase the thing in the first place. This is not inevitable, and I know of a few good racing dogs that are also good workers, but there are a lot more who do either one or the other.

Catching the Sitter

Once your dog has established her running style, you will be able to help her to catch. If she needs a lot of ground to turn in, you won't be giving her the rabbit by the hedge; if she is not particularly fast, or her stamina is wanting, long slips are not the best for her. Taking the sitter rabbit, by day or night, is an art that any dog can master, though, and is not particularly difficult to teach. The dog's eye sees movement easily, but the camouflaged rabbit sitting still is difficult for her, so she must work on trust. I have a specific whistle that means 'sitter', and the dog knows to look on the ground when she hears this whistle. I send her down the beam, giving a single 'stop' whistle and then the 'sitter' whistle. In addition, I hold the lamp high to direct the beam downwards, and rock the light to try to keep the rabbit sitting. The closer the dog is to the rabbit, the faster I do my pulsed whistle. One of my colleagues angles the lamp to the side that he wants the dog to move, and then returns the beam to the rabbit.

Rabbits that squat in the beam never do it twice, and as the season progresses, you have fewer opportunities with sitters because you have either caught them or taught them. Unless you are lucky enough to come across a tract of land that has not been lamped for two or three rabbit generations, sitters will be few and seldom. Rabbits learn from other rabbits, so when you put on the beam and old, wise rabbits run for safety, young rabbits will copy their example and run as well. Wild rabbits rarely live more than a year or two, so this is the kind of break that you will need if the rabbits on your land have become lamp-shy. Of course, you will lose permission land if you don't touch it for a year, and your rabbits will simply become educated to someone else's lamp. This means striking a compromise, being quick on the reflexes with land you lamp often, and if you get an area of untouched land, make the most of your first few trips before the rabbits learn the meaning of the bright light. People have different opinions regarding the use of a red filter on a lamp: some swear by it and always use one, others (myself included) find that quarry rapidly learns that red light is as dangerous as white.

To return to the sitter: the first few times, take your dog on a slip right up to the sitting rabbit, and when you are very near, use the noise or whistle that you will use thereafter when you want her to realize that she must look on the ground for a crouching rabbit. If the rabbit jumps up and runs, slip the dog. If it continues to squat – and you can pick some rabbits up in your hands, so tightly do they sit – be patient with your most infuriating dog that is looking everywhere but at the rabbit, and put her nose right on it. She can smell it all right, but not see it. Once she realizes where to look when you make that noise, you are almost there. The day that everything connects and she picks her first sitter is a day for celebration – break out the chocolate biscuits.

Using the Slip

When you start lamping, always use a slip because you need to impress upon your dog that you choose the rabbits – she doesn't. A headstrong young dog that fails to obey you will lose a lot of rabbits, and there will be times that you do not want a particular rabbit run for reasons that you know and she doesn't. It might be near a road, or a rubbish tip, or hidden farm machinery, or it might be one of the black ones that you have been told to leave alone. Some dogs, as they mature, are perfectly behaved off the slip, and can be directed onto the right rabbit without ever disobeying. Others are so keen that they pelt down the beam whenever the lamp is switched on, blindly trusting that there will be a rabbit at the end of it. Never be ashamed to use a slip if it serves your purpose, or be persuaded that 'all' lurchers should work without one. You are working a real flesh-and-blood dog with her own ways and foibles,

you are out to catch rabbits and to enjoy yourselves, and there is nothing achieved except needless misery if you and she are constantly at odds with each other because she doesn't match the standards of someone else. If she is keen to get on with her job, how much of a fault is that? It is far more difficult to persuade a reluctant dog to hunt than it is to restrain an eager one. So use a slip if it leaves you free to concentrate on the job in hand, and never mind anyone else.

One Dog or Two?

Lamping rabbits is undoubtedly best using just one dog. Running two dogs together can be done well and certainly increases the catch rate, but unless the dogs are exceptional, it doesn't do a lot for the state of the rabbit by the time it comes to hand. When I first started lurcher work, it was with a mother and daughter team, where the senior dog always retrieved the catch no matter which one had actually caught it. Both bitches were soft-mouthed, and rabbits came back completely unmarked. I have never seen two dogs work like it since, but at the time I was too much of a novice to realize just how special these dogs were. Normally, if you run two dogs together, they will dispute possession of the rabbit once it has been caught, and may even cease to retrieve altogether. There is also a very real risk of collision and injury. More than two dogs running together on a rabbit is a farce, though worth watching just the once to realize what a waste of dog power and rabbit meat it can be. Letting a sapling run with an older dog will really annoy the trained dog, especially if she is trying to retrieve to hand, but the young dog is niggling away trying to grab the rabbit.

*Typical Collie
lurcher mark.*

However, there will be times when you want to lamp in company, and the best way is to take turns and have the acting dog well away from the resting dog when she is lamped. That way, you won't foul up the retrieving of either dog. If the dogs are biddable enough, it is possible to lamp two by slipping them alternately, but most dogs are too keen to make this anything other than a chore. One of my friends, who lamps purebred Greyhounds, leaves one in the car while he takes the other, then changes dogs. Although he always muzzles the one that is left in the car, he has come back to some interesting modifications from time to time. By far the best arrangement is one handler to one dog.

So why go out in company? It is a good way to gee up a dog that is not working to her best ability, or to teach a new dog old tricks. It is a nice way to share your permission land with someone who has none, or to show someone the ropes who is new to lamping. If the land is swarming with rabbits and the landowner wants results

fast, more than one dog will mean more catching power, for one can rest as another runs. If I am lamping new land and the landowner or keeper does not know me well, I like to take him out with me so that he can see for himself how the dogs and I conduct ourselves. I recollect a night when my dog ran a rabbit right through a flock of sheep and then returned through the flock looking neither right nor left. The landowner was so impressed by this display of stock-steadiness that I acquired another 1,500 acres of permission on the spot.

The Skill Factor

I have heard lamping described as requiring no skill, being boring, the sort of thing a trained gibbon could do, unsporting, or very good sport, and the best fun you can have with your clothes on. Which is right? All of them. It depends on the land that you have available and the dog you are working.

Like many good things in life, lamping is easy to do badly. If you have large areas of rabbit-infested land to lamp, you can be as careless as you like and still come home having had a lot of fun and with a fair catch. However, if you only have a few hundred acres of small fields, if the rabbits are lamp-shy, or hunted by other means, or hunted so well that there aren't all that many, then you are going to have to develop some fieldcraft. We all read that the ideal lamping night is one that is pitch dark with a smattering of rain and a decent wind. When you get one of these, cancel all engagements and lamp for all you're worth, for there will be no better. If you wait for these conditions, though, you will get precious little lamping unless you live in one of those bleak and beautiful parts of the country where the wind blows all year round, and there is no reflected glow from street lights and housing estates to stop the darkness in its tracks.

Mostly, you will be lamping in less than ideal conditions, and will have to be content with catches in single figures rather than the wheelbarrow loads that you hear about from people who do their lamping in the pub. You are catching rabbits by night not because the light inconveniences or frightens them – it doesn't – but because at night they feed further away from cover, and so your dog has a better chance of picking them up before they make it home. You will never see a rabbit run as fast as the rabbit which is fifty yards from shelter with a longdog up its chuff. The fifty-yard rabbit is very, very hard to catch, so you want to find him further from home if you possibly can. As your dog becomes wiser, she will learn to catch rabbits much closer to home, and you will learn how best to place her. Ideally, you need to lamp where you've been, not where you are going, and place yourself between the rabbit and where he wants to run, but sometimes the lie of the field won't permit this. Once the rabbit has put in his first turn, all the rules change anyway.

If the ideal night in terms of weather does not coincide with the right phase of the moon, you can still lamp as long as you move quietly. A light but windy night will bag you more rabbits than a still, dark one, and rain is wonderful because the rabbits sit more tightly, there is cloud cover, and enough noise to mask any that you are making. If it has rained all day and continues to rain into the night, there will be more rabbits out than if a wet night follows a dry evening, because in the latter case, the rabbits will have fed at dusk and gone back downstairs to watch television. If you were to take a walk around the same fields night after night, you would become aware of a great variation in the numbers of rabbits out, not only because of current conditions, but due to the conditions several hours previously. Sometimes a strong whiff of fox will tell you that you have timed it badly for this field, and I have inadvertently lamped rabbits for foxes more than once. Watch and learn what is going on around you, and put it all to good use: some people lamp for years and never learn rabbit sense.

Rabbits by Day

The daytime rabbit is very much harder to catch, and if your rabbiting opportunities are limited to day work above ground, you will enjoy great sport but not such a full game bag. Daytime rabbits are seldom far from safety, and the dog won't have so many chances for a catch. What you will develop is some fine game-finding techniques.

First, find your rabbits. Areas of shelter such as reed beds are ideal, for the lurcher can use her nose, and won't be hampered by having to negotiate painful areas of thick thorn scrub. Some lurchers quickly develop the knack of pouncing on a seated rabbit; others take longer. Here we have the mystery of 'nose'.

However your lurcher is bred, she will have a better nose than any human. Using it is another matter, rather like some very intelligent people who never learn to think. I have seen purebred Whippets, Greyhounds, Deerhounds and Salukis all using their noses well enough to make a good job of finding quarry in covert or underground. I regularly hunt both a pack of lurchers and a mixed pack of terriers and lurchers, and every time the lurchers do the job easily. The secret unfolds simply through taking your time.

When you take your lurcher out, let her put her nose to the ground and find scent to follow. Take her to where the rabbits were sitting until you climbed the stile into the field, and let her follow their scent to the bury. Take her into woodland, where scent clings to damp leafmould, take her to the fox earth and let her sniff round that. There are those that forbid a lamping dog ever to put her nose to the ground, but she will soon learn not to bother with her nose when out lamping, for the action is faster and easier by following the beam. The quickest way to show a lurcher nose work is to let her follow another dog using its nose well, which need not be another lurcher. But be warned: a gazehound that has learned to use her nose is a double handful to control, for when she loses sight of her quarry she has the ability to track it until she pushes it out again. All of mine do this, and believe me, I have had some work to do on the obedience training. The strain I breed is outstanding for gamefinding, and one of my pleasures is hunting out woodland with the lurcher pack, which

Watching the nets.

sifts silently and delicately through the undergrowth with the persistence of a foxhound pack. Drive we don't have, and drive we don't need, for it would be easy to draw over quarry that way. Nor do I need to lieu them in or cheer them on, for I know that they will draw the wood thoroughly on their own without any encouragement from me. But they know to come to my 'holloa' if a fox breaks, and if we don't have the crash of hound music to thrill our souls, we certainly have a chase that lacks for nothing.

Hunting out fairly open country with the lurcher pack is good, but when it comes to hedgerow work or thickets of bramble, you need a short-legged dog with a thick jacket. Working terriers and lurchers together can be fantastic sport or a total disaster, and I've had both. No matter how good your lurcher is at covert-hunting, if she is inside sniffing out game, she will not be in a position to course it when it breaks. Therefore the little ones go into covert while the lurchers mark where the action

is on the outside, and, with luck, they will be well placed for a course when the terriers achieve a bolt. And this is where it can all go completely wrong.

Whatever is in there getting quarry out must be trained to come off it as soon as it bolts. The first time I worked my lurcher with terriers was disastrous, for my good bitch had a series of catches ripped out of her mouth by an undisciplined rabble of terriers. Lurchers just will not stand for that sort of treatment, so I called a halt to the whole sorry business, losing a friend and a large tract of hunting ground in the process. Some years later, I was again offered the chance to work my lurchers with terriers, and, bristling with misgivings, I agreed. This particular area of land had been really frustrating to work, as the lurchers were finding plenty of game but were unable to penetrate and work the thorn thicket, though they certainly tried. However, once the terriers were brought in it became a different story. These particular terriers had been

Bolt imminent!

trained by a roughshooting man, and so had been taught to come off quarry once it had bolted. The lurchers were able to do their job without a string of hollering terriers hacking after them. Also, with the terriers owned and worked by someone else, I could concentrate wholly on the lurchers. There are people who can handle both, and very well too, but it's certainly no easy task.

The way the terriers' owner and I hunt is like this: we take either side of a hedgerow or thicket. The old silver brindle lurcher is almost always the first to find, and she freezes on point. Terriers come bustling up to enter at the appropriate place, and there is much snuffling and crackling, while lurchers circle outside following what's happening. Presently the black terrier yaps excitedly and out shoots a rabbit, to be either deftly scooped up by a lurcher, rolled over by the gun, or to escape honourably to run another day. You need steady dogs and an absolutely safe snapshooter for this game, but with the right ingredients you can have a marvellous day's hunting.

Terriers have their own agenda, their philosophy of life being: eat it, fight it, **** it or roll in it, and going to ground is high on their list of pleasurable pastimes. If you do run your lurcher with terriers, do a recce first, and satisfy yourself that the ground you are intending to work does not contain anything that will be of too much interest to the terriers, and that the terriers themselves are not going to give your lurcher grief. Never, ever hunt with an unknown person carrying a gun. It just isn't worth it.

The single lurcher can be a very efficient pot-filler, especially if she has trained you to carry a stout stick with which to poke about in the bushes. My old bitch used to enter covert and drive game towards me, and did she ever get irritated when I missed it, which was mostly. Later, when I bred her, and ended up running two pups on with my own as their new owner was bang in the middle of haymaking, then harvest, she taught the pups to hunt using exactly the same method. The result was a mixed blessing: three pups that knew how to find and catch, and that hunted like fiends from the nest, but that were the very devil to discipline, having had such an early taste of honey. Try not to do it that way! But watch your lurcher when you take her out, watch her body language and what she is telling you. Lurchers are terrific communicators, if you only take the trouble to observe and interpret their actions. The more time you spend with your dog, the more you will come to understand each other. She will become a real lurcher, an opportunist hunter and pot-filler. And you, whatever the weather, will wear a coat or waistcoat with rather deep pockets.

Ferreting

Ferreting with a trained lurcher is a real pleasure. Only one dog should be used for this job, or else it will lead to tears, but a good ferreting lurcher is more help than a human companion. Training is straightforward, and any cross of lurcher can make a good ferreting dog.

Introducing Your Dog to Ferrets

First, she must be absolutely safe with ferrets. There are people who like to introduce a lurcher pup to ferret kits over a bowl of milk, but I don't use this method for several reasons. One is that I never managed to have both pup and kits at the same time. Also, some animals are possessive about their food and can get quarrelsome if expected to share, and I rarely give animals milk anyway, as it is a strong laxative and not at all good for them. This being said, many people use this method, and are convinced that it is the best way. Perhaps it is: I have never had the slightest trouble in breaking lurchers to ferrets, but have never succeeded in breaking ferrets to lurchers. Therefore, I aim for mutual respect on all sides (including me), and I have never had a ferret touched by a dog. I do go to great lengths to make sure that my dogs don't get nipped by ferrets, as few dogs will stand for that, and no ferret would survive the return match.

I start with the dog on a lead, and the ferret in my hand. Let them have a good look at each other, and let them sniff, but don't allow the ferret to nip, and tell the dog 'No – leave it' if she tries to lunge at the ferret. When they are comfortable about each other's presence, progress to a stage where the dog is tied up or on a lead, and the ferret is allowed to run about near her on a harness and line, and then loose the dog and let the ferret play near her, discouraging any attempt at contact. When you are satisfied about this, loose them both in a confined area, supervising them the whole time that they are together. Some dogs, especially terriers, can be unreliable about ferrets all their lives, but a fair few lurcher and ferret relationships become actively trusting and friendly. Don't take any risks with a strange or unproven dog near your ferrets, though – many a ferret death has been preceded by the words, 'I'm sure he'll be all right'. And if your dog is very ferret-friendly, mind her with a ferret that is not her own, in case she approaches in trust and gets badly bitten. She may well not be ferret-proof thereafter.

Marking Rabbit Buries

Once the dog is steady to ferrets, she must mark rabbit buries. She probably does this already, so you must learn to interpret what she is telling you. When she sniffs at rabbit holes, she can tell not only if there are rabbits within, but whether there is one or several, deep in or close to the surface and ready to bolt. She will communicate this knowledge to you, and it is up to you to understand her. Some dogs look at you in a certain way, some point, some stare into the bury and wag their tails – observe her carefully and soon you will be able to recognize the signals. This is one area of training that you do not reward with a pat, or with praise or titbit, for if she thinks that the act of marking pleases you, then she will false mark, that is, adopt a 'rabbit within' posture at every rabbit hole, because she thinks that that is what you want. The only reward for a mark should be to put in a ferret, so that she knows ferret in equals rabbit out. This will give you a first-class marking dog for ever after. If you lose a lot of rabbits when you start teaching your dog to lamp, you will lose even more in the early days of ferreting, but look upon it as an exercise in 'speculate to accumulate'. Once your dog has marking mastered, you will be moving into the first division for rabbit catching.

If you can, choose a small bury with a lot of field around it. This is easier said than done, so you may have to compromise, in which case a large open bury in a large open space will serve your purpose better than a small bury surrounded by hedgerow. Let your dog mark, and put in the

Letting the bury settle after netting.

ferret (an experienced ferret, please, for one novice at a time is quite enough). When the rabbit bolts, the dog will likely miss it. Whistle her straight back to the bury, because she must not hunt on. The more time she spends peering down destination rabbit holes, the more rabbits will be bolted by your ferret to a dog that isn't there. Be patient; she will soon learn where the action is.

The first few times, keep her on a slip until the rabbit bolts, and only loose her when the rabbit is clear of the bury. Some rabbits exit like rockets, others hop slowly to the bury entrance and peer about before they commit themselves to leaving, and you don't want your dog to lunge at these and frighten them into bobbing back under. See in your mind's eye the made dog waiting, trembling, for the unwary coney to creep slowly out of the bury, neatly into the nettle clump and out again, ready to make a break for the woods. Once the rabbit is out of cover and clear of the bury, the dog strikes and picks up, with a

minimum of effort but with skill and control in spades. This is what you are teaching your sapling now, and won't she just learn fast!

Placing the Nets

Once you have bolted some rabbits for your dog, and she has cottoned on to what a smashing little chap the ferret is, put a few purse nets down, but don't net all the holes. Some people like a dog to leave a netted rabbit completely, others prefer the netted rabbit to be pinned until they can reach it, and I am one of these. If the ground is too hard to get the pegs in firmly, or you've only got half the rabbit in the net, the dog that will hold the rabbit is worth gold. A purse-netted rabbit doesn't half ping about and will get loose before long, but a good lurcher will hold it tenderly until you can get there. Murphy's Law of Ferreting decrees that nothing happens and then everything does, so anything that can stop a rabbit escaping when you have one under each arm and one in each hand is well worth a few rabbit escapees in the early stages. Incidentally, if you do have a mass exodus of rabbits and run out of hands, don't do what a friend of mine did, and pop a rabbit between your thighs. Rabbits can and do deliver a nasty bite, and this one did. Luckily it was face down, but the sweat broke out on his brow and still does when he recalls the incident.

After you have netted the holes, but before you put the ferret in, take your dog around the bury and gently dissuade her if she paws or tries to dislodge the nets. Nets are not to be touched, and it is extremely irritating to work with a dog, however good in other ways, that makes you keep resetting the nets. You have taught her to 'Leave it' from when she was tiny, and now you reap the value of those early obedience lessons, for she knows exactly what you mean, and will probably only need one lesson at this. Then, ferret down, dog on slip. If you get a bolter, let the dog run after it; if you have a netted rabbit, tell her to leave it if you want it left, or let her pounce on it if you want it held. Some dogs pin with their feet, others with their mouths, but it doesn't matter which she does, as long as she doesn't crunch the rabbit, or pull the lot up, peg and all, and run off with it. Yes, I have seen it happen, but if she is on the slip, she isn't going far, and you can nip that one in the bud before it becomes a distressing habit. As soon as she has pegged the rabbit, take it and praise her lavishly. Don't let her mouth the catch once it is dead and laid out, it is yours now not hers, but bring her quietly back to the bury. If she courses and catches, preferably to retrieve to you, don't rush to snatch her rabbit off her, but take it tactfully with much praise. You might lose a few rabbits while you are doing this,

but with ferreting, the dog knows the action is centred on the bury, just as with lamping that it happens with the lamp, which is the incentive you use to get her to return to you after she has caught or lost the rabbit. This is why the discipline is so tight with these two activities, compared with bushing, where the dog finds her own quarry rather than looking to you to produce it.

Now you can progress to netting all the rabbit holes and dispensing with the slip. In the early stages of training, when your youngster may have a short attention span, it is easier on both of you if you tie her up while you are netting, rather than subjecting her to the control of a 'down–stay' for half an hour or more. Later, you will find that she loiters by the bury in happy anticipation of what comes next. What you don't want is for her to get into the habit of sloping off to do some free-lancing, and possibly vanishing for some time. If you don't want her to touch netted rabbits at all, leave a couple of exit holes uncovered so that she gets the chance of a run, otherwise she will become very frustrated, then unco-operative, then disobedient. Ferreting should be fun for her, too, and if she likes to carry a rabbit back to the car afterwards, well, why not?

As your dog develops her ferreting skills, you will be astounded at how much she can tell you. She will stand over the bury or tiptoe across it, following the action, ears flicking. She can hear far better than you what is going on underground, and is feeling the vibration with her feet as well. Some lurchers develop the knack of snatching up a fleeing rabbit as it leaves, some will pinpoint the position of the ferret, and some will even dig to where the ferret is holding a rabbit (no matter how good friends dog and ferret are, it is advisable for you to take over the digging when this happens). Some lurchers become so good at following what is going on underground that you don't need to net at all, because she will have her mouth in the right place every time. She won't learn these skills overnight, and nor will you learn quickly how best to make use of her skills, but given time and plenty of practice, your lurcher will become a real asset on a ferreting trip. And she will be a most worthy companion well into her dotage, for a ferreting lurcher can still do her job long after her speed has gone.

Foxes

Not every lurcher will make a good fox dog. She needs to be high-couraged and totally committed to her task. Many lurchers will course a fox but not tackle it, leading their owners to delude themselves that they have a foxing lurcher. If that lurcher is not putting some bends into the fox, she isn't trying.

There are three main ways of taking fox using lurchers: bolting them from their earths using terriers (like ferreting, only bigger), pushing them out of covert with dogs, beaters, or both and then coursing them, and lamping. The fox over fifty yards is very fast indeed. I am always amused when I hear people hold forth about foxing who claim that foxes don't run fast: like all quarry, the fox runs as fast as he is pressed. A fox with a pack of hounds behind him will toddle or lope in a steady, unhurried manner. Hounds are simply an inconvenience that he wishes to distance himself from, and he does not perceive himself in danger until it is too

late. A fox chased by a pet dog will exert himself just enough to stay ahead of the dog. A fox chased by a longdog will go like the blazes.

Foxes bolted from earth or covert know exactly where they are going and aim to get there unimpeded. Nothing is quieter than a fox that does not wish to be heard – he can slip out right beside you, and you may turn in time to catch a flash of red, but you won't hear him. The lurcher can be on him in a very few strides, and it is all over. That doesn't mean that the fox is slow, just that as he wasn't expecting you to be there with a longdog, he tried to sneak away to safety rather than run at full tilt. The terrier is an annoyance to the fox, so he aims to leave the noise behind and unless you have been careless and noisy outside the earth, he will not be expecting that anyone is eagerly awaiting his departure. As with ferreting, if the fox thinks that outside is dangerous, he will opt to stay inside, and then he must be dug to. Once you start digging, he may well change his mind and bolt, but the lurcher that can get a clear run has a very good chance of connecting. The fox is a master at using the contours of the land to his advantage, and will weave around every obstacle trying to foil the dog. You won't believe how a fox can turn until you see one being worked by a persistent lurcher.

You may choose to use two dogs to shorten the odds, as they will work the fox between them until one can pick him up. More than two dogs, however, can get in each others' way. There are plenty of first-class, single-handed fox dogs about, but I tend to work two smallish bitches rather than one big one. The smaller dogs turn better, while the larger dogs have more power and weight to effect the kill. I have

Giving fair law.

also had a lot of success working a small bitch to a large dog, the bitch doing the work and taking the turns out of the fox until the time is right for the dog to intercept the quarry with one decisive, crushing bite. The important thing is to work within your dog's capabilities and limitations: if he is fast and strong but doesn't turn so nimbly, he will either need a smaller, nippier companion or more space in which to do his work. If she is nimble and fiery but small of jaw, a big fellow helping will make the job easier. Look at that dead fox – see the long jaws and the backward-hooked canine teeth. They don't grow those for eating worms and beetles with. A fox can deliver a punishing bite, and it is better that he never gets the chance to. As with all animals, the general assumption is that the female is deadlier than the male; a vixen presents a smaller, more agile target, and is generally reckoned to be more fiery than a dog fox.

Lamping with Foxes

Lamping foxes with lurchers is very different from lamping rabbits. Your quarry is much more wary. You can squeak in foxes to you by using a variety of noises supposed to imitate a rabbit, hare, or even fox – some people are artists at this – or there are commercial fox calls that can be bought, but a fox once squeaked in and missed is a fox that has been educated and is unlikely to come in to a squeak again. You can bait a field with carrion – the older and smellier the better – and sit in wait for the foxes that will be attracted to it, or you can simply lamp for rabbits and take your foxes on an opportunist basis. Nothing squeaks in a fox better than a squealing rabbit in the jaws of a soft-mouthed lurcher, and lampers are often trailed by foxes. When first training my fawn bitch to the lamp, she was followed up the beam by a fox as she returned with her rabbit, but as she hadn't been entered to fox, and was only just getting her lamping discipline established, I had to let it go. The farmer would not have been impressed, had he known, for he was losing poultry to a fox, but my trained bitch was not with me, and I wasn't going to risk ruining the young one by premature entering.

When lamping rabbits, you can take certain liberties with the wind and the moon, but a fox must not have any idea that you are there. He will approach using every bit of cover that he can, coming windward of you if the land allows, and if he once gets a whiff of you, he'll be off. There can be no smoking when lamping, or wearing smoky clothes from two hours in the pub, no eating peppermints, no wearing aftershave or scent, not when hunting for rabbits and certainly not for foxes. Some people like to call the fox in on the red filter, while training their dog to run the white light only; others use the white beam throughout. However, you can be absolutely certain that if the fox has been educated to any particular system, he won't fall for it again.

Ideally, you want the fox as close in as possible, and as far as you can get him from covert. A fox coursed hard for fifty yards will have had much of the fight taken out of him; his brush goes up as he swerves again, and the lurcher picks him up. I have seen an exceptionally fast lurcher scorch up to his fox and close an eighty-yard gap with the fox running away, but many would be unable to catch at that sort of distance. Remember that your job is pest control, and that your fox and dog must connect in such a manner that neither is caused suffering. This means that if your dog pins rather than kills her fox, you must be prepared to administer the coup de grâce as quickly as possible. If you are selling pelts – almost impossible at time of writing, but the market comes and goes – you need a dog that pins. Secure the fox and despatch it quickly, if your dog has not already done so. The fox can freeze into a catatonic state when caught, making the job easy, or he can thrash and spit like a captured demon.

Terrier and lurcher team: a lethal combination.

Be above reproach in your despatch of any quarry, being sure to do the job swiftly and humanely. As he has to die, let him die well. None of us enjoys killing, but it is a part of the job that has to be done, and done properly.

Always be sure that it is indeed a fox that you have on the lamp before you send your dog out. Muntjac deer or a big farm cat can look like a fox on occasion, and once I saw a pair of eyes down by the hedge and couldn't identify the owner at all, not until it said 'baa' and tottered off to find its Mum. Never lamp on eyes alone; err on the side of caution rather than cause a tragic accident. Also, a lurcher entered to deer, cat or lamb in this manner will prove very hard to correct.

A fox held in the beam of the lamp will quickly look and move away, and will be difficult to follow when he does. For the most part, if he is going to come in, he will do so quickly, and if he is not, he will find a vantage point and watch you from it. One very frustrating fox watched us from the end of a fence line for over half an hour, clearly wanting to come in, but not daring to. The following day, we found out why: we had been crouching next to the pulled-out rabbit bury in which she had her cubs! She was a troublesome poultry-killer and duly dealt with, along with her family.

Entering Your Dog to Fox

Properly done, foxing with lurchers is very efficient and humane, and in areas where a rifle cannot safely be used, or the Hunt cannot operate, is an invaluable method of control. Correctly entering your lurcher is vital. It is one occasion where I always use a made dog, for not all lurchers recognize the fox as legitimate quarry. One of the bravest fox dogs that I have ever seen in action made amorous advances to a dog fox during her first oestrus season. He was neither amused nor aroused, crouching and spitting before the posturing bitch. Later, when she was old enough, she entered to fox with an intent that seemed totally out of keeping with such a gentle bitch. What is old enough? I don't expect a lurcher to tackle a fox before she is two, and one of mine didn't get her first fox until she was three, because I couldn't find the right one to start her off until then. She paid for the waiting and now lacks nothing as a fox killer. The right fox is a fox in the right place, under the right circumstances, with a made dog along to help. Having achieved that, there should not be any problems.

If your lurcher is not inclined to the fox job, don't force her. Many lurchers will not face a fox, but do other aspects of their job perfectly well. If you specifically need a foxing lurcher, buy something that is bred for the job, but be aware that she may not be quite so suitable in other spheres. I would suggest a dog with plenty of Deerhound, Saluki, Bull Terrier or Bedlington blood added to Greyhound or Whippet, and preferably with one or both parents proven as foxing dogs. Some foxing lurchers may turn hard-mouthed and, very occasionally, a foxing lurcher may become touchy with small red dogs. Such lurchers know perfectly well that the other is a dog, but seem unable to resist chasing them, so if yours starts to develop such tendencies, be careful.

Hunting on by Scent

If your lurcher has a good nose, you can get problems with her hunting on by scent. There are areas where a solo

The tools for the job: an outstanding fox dog.

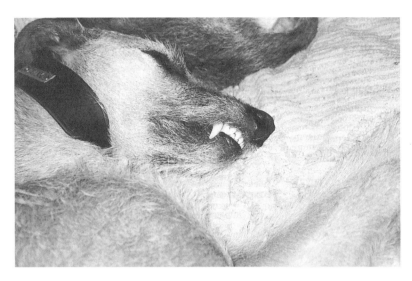

lurcher running hot drag can get away with it, but for the most part landowners and gamekeepers have a keen allergy to unaccompanied lurchers. A fox tracked to its lair by a fast, silent dog is no use to you unless you have that unusual sort of dog that will come back to get you and take you on to the earth. Most will not, and your dog runs the risk of ending her life to a gun, a wire or a car, or being picked up and taken to a Dog Rescue centre, which often put working dogs down straight away. I once bred a bitch that went to a farm home and became something of a fox specialist, adept at following scent when she went unsighted. Returning from one of these jaunts, she happened to cross a field of sheep, and though she did not look at them, the farmer informed her owner that the next time it happened, the dog's grave would be an open ditch. She was rehomed by me, though the story continues with the sheep farmer claiming sheep worried by this lurcher that now in fact no longer lived in the same county. It transpired that the farm's own collie was

killing lambs, but the whole unsavoury story illustrates the problems a free-running lurcher can run in to. This is another reason for starting your dog off on lamped rabbits before you progress to lamped foxes, because then she will be thoroughly drilled in coming back to you once the lamp goes off. I have heard people say that they want their dog to continue to run the fox by scent once it is unsighted: I have dogs that can and will do this by day, and I can assure you that it is the last thing that you want unless you live in a truly remote area, or in the midst of thousands of acres of your own land, or don't care about your dog. Scent hunting of a far-ranging quarry is best left to packs of hounds: they are slower and let you know where they are.

Deer

It is very difficult to find opportunities to work deer legally. In Scotland, using dogs on deer is always illegal. At the time of writing, a dog or dogs may be used on deer in the rest of the UK if the landowner has consented (best in writing), if the work is done by day, that is, no later than one hour after sunset or earlier than one hour before sunrise, if the deer is in season for hunting, or if it has been proven to have been causing serious damage. These are fragile circumstances at best, and it would take very little in terms of legal procedure to wipe them out completely. You do not need a game licence if you are not using a firearm, but there are complexities relating to the sale of the carcase, which is the property of the landowner.

The difficulties are that you cannot tell the dog that something is okay on one farm and not on another, nor can you tell the deer to stay within one landowner's boundary. Again, the law is delicate about whether game found on one person's property and killed on another's belongs to the first landowner or the second, and if you add tenancies and gamekeepers to the equation, it can become very tricky indeed. People who do not suffer the damage to their land can wax very sentimental about Bambi and, while you do not quite get transportation for deer poaching any more, the law will be hard on you and harder on your dog, which may well be confiscated. Dogs taken into custody under such circumstances are very unlikely to come home again.

Muntjac

The deer is a natural quarry for any breed of dog, and most will wed to it with frightening enthusiasm. The Saluki was bred for thousands of generations as a gazelle hound, and both these and Deerhound crosses take to the job without any encouragement. German Shepherd crosses are very efficient as well. Muntjac deer, not a native species, are solitary dwellers, and much more plentiful than is generally realized, for they favour thick, thorny covert and are shy in habit. They breed all year round, making a close season irrelevant, can be a confounded nuisance to farmers, and dress out to a surprisingly fleshy carcase. They are well-armed, with stabbing antlers and large canine teeth, and if they decide to fight it out with a dog in covert, can make a lot of noise and do a deal of damage.

Roe and Fallow

Roe are the next size up, seen mostly in pairs or singles, very plentiful and bold, superb eating, and an easy target for a lurcher because of their tendency to run in circles. They are native to Britain, unlike Fallow, the next size up. The 'wild' Fallow found in this country are park escapees, and enjoy an unusual status in law as they are presumed to belong to somebody. Fallow live in herds, and it is an education to see a dog set the herd moving and then cut out one deer that is weaker than the rest. This is pure Nature, undiluted with sentiment or domesticity, the survival of the fittest. Fallow will take your dog a long, long way, across roads and into all sorts of hazards. Although quite a small dog can pull one, it takes a strong dog to hold one, and if you are not on hand quickly to finish the job, your dog may receive a lot of punishment.

Sika and Red

Sika (imported) and Red (native) deer are our largest breeds and, sadly, these two crossbreed well. The venison is good enough, but can be rank on occasion, and the smaller breeds eat better. You would need more than one big, strong, capable dog to tackle these, and a humane kill would not be easy to effect, unless you were right on hand with them. Purebred Scottish Deerhounds were easily capable of a quick kill on Red deer, in the days when this was legal in Scotland, but the law has changed and so have the Deerhounds. Red deer hunted with packs of scenting hounds are brought to bay and then shot at point-blank range; the hounds do not touch the deer at all. I am rather inclined to think that this and deerstalking are the best ways of dealing with the big fellows, now that the noble Deerhound may no longer do her historical job in the land of her creation.

Taking the Deer

The entered lurcher will use one of several methods to take her deer. Some (especially Saluki-bred ones) jump on their backs to drop them, then go for the throat. Others (the Deerhound speciality) jump up and catch hold of the back of the neck, which breaks as the deer goes over. Some dogs pull the deer by gripping just above the hock, some will run beside the deer and shoulder-charge it when both forelegs are off the ground, finishing the job with a throat hold in each case. You will read about poaching gangs using packs of dogs, where the deer suffer horribly, and their despicable actions are quoted to taint all deer work. In truth, one or two dogs who know what they are about get the job done so quickly that the deer is dead in seconds, and the carcase almost undamaged. However, people who avidly watch television films of gazelles being brought down by big cats will be beside themselves at the thought of a British deer being caught by a dog, so no matter how much permission you have, or how well your dog can do her job, you are best to keep the matter between yourself and your landowner.

Hearsay has it that the dog used on deer will become a sheep worrier, but this is

Three-legged fox; a necessary cull of a poultry killer.

nonsense, as long as your dog has been properly stockbroken. Your dog can tell the difference between sheep and deer just as well as you can, and will continue to be reliable with livestock no matter how much work she does on the big stuff.

I once had a lot of permission on Roe, and an outstanding bitch to take them. The problem was that she wed to her quarry with such conviction that she would even break off from ferreting if a Roe passed us. It was impossible for her to understand that her considerable talents were only required in one place, and we had some awkward moments. I would not want such a dog again, though I could have named my price for her. I loved her dearly, and kept her to the end of her days, but it is my opinion, given the difficulty of obtaining permission on deer, and the enormous potential for grief when it goes wrong, that we are all best advised to steady our dogs to deer and to buy our venison.

Hares

The brown hare and the blue or mountain hare present two very different challenges to the lurcher. The brown hare is reckoned to be the finest of all quarry and is certainly an amazing animal. Given fair law (eighty plus yards start), she can run rings around the fittest of Greyhounds, and does so at every coursing meet. For running the brown hare, the most usual cross is the Saluki/Greyhound, using the Saluki for stamina and the Greyhound for speed. Each has a very different coursing technique: the Greyhound powers up to her hare and puts in a dazzling display of turns, while the Saluki settles in behind her quarry, waiting for it to make a mis-

take. The Greyhound has to do her job quickly, for she burns out very fast, but the Saluki can afford to take her time. Greyhound coursing is won or lost in around a minute, but four minutes is not uncommon for Salukis and their crosses. The hare goes no faster than she needs. Watch one coursed by a terrier or a Labrador – she won't even trouble to flatten her ears as she skips away. Put a fast dog behind her, and her ears are pressed flat as she pulls out a repertoire of jinks and turns which can faze all but the very best dogs.

Hare country varies, with their distribution being rather ragged, although hares do thrive where the conditions are right. Agrochemicals and foxes are their main enemies, and where these are controlled you will find your hares. Organized coursing is the saviour of the brown hare, for it is the big sporting estates that provide a sympathetic environment for her. Sadly, the poaching gangs play a big part in the extermination of the hare from certain areas, for they course her by day and lamp her by night, all year round. Not only does this have a catastrophic effect on hare numbers, it gives people the impression that all coursing is illegal, and that it is fieldsports' supporters who behave so. Those opposed to country sports would do better to understand that the real threats to such as the hare are the despicable poaching louts and not the fieldsports' supporters, who put as much back into the land as they take out.

The average owner of an average lurcher will not, however, course with fair law, but will allow the dog to hunt up the hare and then run her. This is good sport, favouring the wise dog as much as the fast one, and the odds are heavy on the side of the hare. This is natural selection, too, as all hunting with dogs is, because the hare caught by your lurcher will be one that is weaker or more foolish than the rest. It is an exceptional lurcher that can catch a fair-law hare on a regular basis, but a lurcher that can find her hare in a seemingly empty field and either lift her out of her seat before she runs, or course her, will provide royal sport. There can be few better sights than a good dog after a good hare, watching the hare spin around on her hindlegs to catch the dog flatfooted, or leaping clean over her pursuer's head to land going flat out in the other direction. Whatever the outcome, be it a proud, panting dog with the hare at her feet, or the hare scooting to safety having run the dog unsighted, the brown hare is a superb quarry, lovely to see around, matchless to course, and delicious to eat. What more could you want?

Hares are sensitive to changes in agriculture, very prone to fox predation, especially of leverets, and apt to sudden population crashes that we don't fully understand. Nowadays, the brown hare is most plentiful on sporting estates that support coursing, and so afford her the food and shelter she needs as well as protection from foxes.

The blue hare's distribution is in the higher and northernmost districts, and she is a very different stamp of quarry. A nimble dog is required, for she will run some punishing country, using every inch of it to throw off her pursuers. The granite outcrop and hidden fall is home to this hare of the heather, and she will easily go to ground if the opportunity coincides with the need. Her culinary qualities are supposed to be less good than the brown hare, but as I have never eaten a mountain hare, I cannot comment on this. Within her distribution, she is plentiful, and a good sporting quarry in her own right, even if she has not the glamorous image of the brown hare. Your lurcher will have to work hard to catch either hare, and you should be proud of her when she does.

Other Game

Feather

Though the foregoing are the prime quarry for lurchers, you will meet a miscellany of others as you go about your work. Most lurchers will work feather with great gusto, pheasants being especially liked. If you intend to work your dog on sporting estates, rough-hunting or in the beating line, she will need to learn that pheasant, partridge and the like should be flushed but not pegged (many gundogs could do with learning this as well). Sitting gamebirds are supposed not to carry much scent, but they certainly carry enough for a lurcher, mine having flushed a very varied tally of feather, including snipe. To see a lurcher leap after a flushed pheasant and land with it neatly folded between her long jaws is a guilty pleasure; lucky for me that on the occasions when it has been witnessed by the people responsible for the pheasants, they have been so impressed by the catch that they have been forgiving! Remember that your dog has no comprehension of close season, so do not give her the opportunity of disturbing ground-nesting birds. Many gundogs take a lot of teaching before they will retrieve pigeon, because the loose feathers are troublesome to them. All my lurchers catch pigeon, and even the reluctant retrievers will bring them back before making a great fuss about the feathers on their lips. I remember a

A good morning's work.

certain puppy raiding the gamebag and carrying several pigeons into the house, to eat their heads and pluck their bodies lavishly on the sofa. I found the loose feathers troublesome, too.

Squirrels

Squirrels are a great favourite with lurchers. Some get bitten by their first squirrel, and if you have examined a squirrel's teeth, you will understand the force of the bite. They will never be bitten thereafter. Lurchers make very agile squirrelling dogs, and can be as good as terriers on a drey-poling outing. My Bedlington cross recently ran straight up the side of the church to collect a squirrel. Beware of squirrel fleas, though – soft-shelled and red, they bite anyone and anything, and I have got into the habit of leaving squirrel carcases to cool and lose their fleas before I take them home for the ferrets.

Mink

Lurchers will hunt mink eagerly, but are disadvantaged once the mink are in the water. They will also despatch stoats, though the lingering smell from either of these will make you wish that they had not. I do not work my lurchers intention-ally on these, as I am not sure what effect it would have on their ferret steadiness. It would probably make no difference at all, as lurchers are far from stupid, but I regard terriers and minkhounds as better for such jobs. Rats, however, give good sport, and teach a dog to use her mouth. Remember that rats carry Weil's Disease, which affects both people and dogs, so don't eat your sandwiches with ratty hands. Rat bites should be treated at the end of the ratting session and, if you do a lot of rat work, you might consider having your dog vaccinated against Weil's.

Whatever your quarry, respect it, be above reproach in your treatment of it and of your dog, and above all enjoy your hunting, the reward for all your hard work. The relationship between a dog and her owner, when you work a natural quarry on its own ground, cannot be bettered.

CHAPTER 4

FITNESS

Whether you regard your lurcher as an essential part of your pest-control equipment, a family pet, your best pal, or all of them, she will have to be fit, and I really mean fit, in order to do her job properly. It is sheer cruelty to leave a dog in her kennel or backyard all week and then work her all weekend. You do not 'work her fit', but get her as fit as you can, then start to work her, and see with astonishment just how much fitter she will become. Once she is 'ticking over fit' you can adjust her regime to bring her up to peak fitness for a special occasion, that invitation to go coursing or lamping for a few days with a friend, or even some competitive coursing, and drop her down a few notches to let her system adjust after a spell of really hard work. It is almost as injurious to attempt to keep an animal at peak fitness for a sustained period as it is to work her when she is unfit; the racehorse people call it 'leaving the race on the gallops' when the horse has done too much work in preparation for the race and has peaked at the wrong time. So it is with your dog: if you keep her just below her optimum fitness, you will be able to fine-tune her condition to every bit as delicate a degree as the big-race winner.

Taking proper care of your dog will result in her staying sound and able to work for many more years than if you

Mostly Greyhound; exercised up and down hills such as the one in the background.

Collie / Saluki at peak fitness.

abuse her health and overuse her when she is not quite ready. Few lurchers are required to work all day every day, and those that do had better be Collie or cattle-dog bred. For most, the bursts of activity are short and hard, and that is how the longdog body is designed to work, with its massive heart and lungs, and ample supply of long muscle fibres. The triangle of fitness contains three points of equal importance: good quality food, good quality exercise and good quality rest, and sufficient of each of them.

Feeding

Feeding skills show up the true stockman every time. The dog is a carnivore – just look at those teeth – but needs the vitamins that can only be provided by vegetable matter and the minerals that come with whole-carcase feeding. Anything else is window-dressing: if it doesn't come from carcases or growing greenstuff, it is not a natural diet. However, dogs prove over and over that they can survive and in some cases thrive on other food. There are even people who, out of misguided 'ethics', force their dogs to eat vegetarian or macrobiotic diets, just as there are those who fill their dogs with bread, cakes and human processed food. The dogs continue to live, and in some cases even look healthy, but they will never reach the sparkling good health of which they are capable if they are fed such rubbish on a sustained basis. You need to feed your dog food that is both readily available and convenient to you, and palatable and good for her. There is quite a choice.

Dog food can be commercial wet (packet or tin), commercial dry, raw or cooked flesh, whole carcase feed, table scraps, home-prepared food, or all of them. Each has its problems and its advantages, so let us take a closer look.

Commercial Pet Food

Commercial dog food is easy to obtain and easy to store, and each can or sack comes with a guaranteed nutritional breakdown, which can sometimes be vague – 'cereals', or specific – 'rice'. Each manufacturer will assure you that this food is nutritionally complete and scientifically balanced, and that it is unnecessary, even harmful, to feed your dog one crumb of anything else. Your dog will tell you differently.

There is no such thing as a complete metabolism. Each dog uses its nutrients to a different degree of efficiency, and a food on which some dogs do well will have others looking wretched. Not all dogs cope well with cereals – when, after all, would a wild dog eat them? – and some ingredients in commercial dog foods are common allergens, such as maize, soya and rapeseed oil. It is likely that some of these will have been genetically modified as well, a real Pandora's box. Although in response to informed public opinion, we are now seeing less in the way of artificial colourings and other chemicals in processed dog food, these are still found in some feedstuffs, and are known in susceptible dogs to cause behavioural problems which are similar to those of hyperactive children who react to certain substances. Commercial feed has to contain something in the way of preservatives, and the long-term effects of these are not known. Certain manufacturers even add ingredients specifically to reduce the size and smell of the dog's faeces, which shows just how far we have moved away from the needs of the dog. Dogs that are prone to 'bloat' – intestinal torsion caused by unnatural fermentation of certain foods, and which can kill by causing the gut to kink and die within the dog – can be especially sensitive to cereal and soya. A dog predisposed to diabetes might have the illness triggered by a diet unnaturally high in molasses, which is added to dog food for the sole purpose of making it more palatable. This does beg the question why

Seen as a pup in Chapter 8; racing fit.

the food has to have something unnatural for canines added to it before they will eat it. But to my mind, the biggest unseen problem of commercial dog food is the ease with which we can feed our dogs a diet that is too high in protein.

It is logical to think that a hard-working dog that is producing bursts of maximum energy is going to need a lot of protein, but the metabolism of food into energy is a little more complex than that. In simplistic terms, just as when you burn wood, you get ash, when you burn energy, you produce waste products known as metabolytes. These substances are excreted by the healthy system via urine, sweat glands, lymphatic drainage and so on, but sometimes are produced in such quantity that the body cannot cope. Unlike humans and horses, dogs are not efficient at sweating, so it is the kidneys that come in for most of the extra work. Crystalline deposits form in the long muscle fibres and the joints, sometimes in the kidneys themselves, which lays the ground for arthritic conditions, kidney stones and local muscle spasm. If the kidneys are under stress for prolonged periods, they will eventually begin to malfunction. The build-up of toxic waste products in the dog's system ultimately produces a very sick dog: you will perhaps see that your dog looks and performs below par, but not be able to put your finger on what is wrong. Perhaps you will feed her more protein, to pep her up a bit.

And what is this protein anyway? If your dog-food label states specifically 'chicken' or 'beef' or similar, then, by law, that is what is in the sack or tin. It will include fairly unusual bits such as hoof and feathers, but nothing that wasn't once part of the animals named. However, if the label says 'meat' or 'meat derivatives' you

may be on something of a nutritional sticky wicket. Euthanased pets from veterinary surgeries, full of the drugs that they were treated with prior to their demise, and possibly still wearing their flea collars and enwrapped in their plastic sack shrouds, are processed into some brands of manufactured pet food. You may not wish to feed this to your dog.

How high a protein level is too high? Like everything else, it varies from dog to dog, but I would suggest that you keep to a maintenance diet of around 22 per cent protein, and lower if you can and your dog does well on it. The particularly high protein feeds were designed for huskies in Alaska, and while they may be relevant perhaps for wildfowling dogs in bitter winter conditions, will stir up trouble for the gazehound in the field. I'm not saying that protein is bad, quite the contrary, but it must be fed with care and its effect on your dogs closely observed. I have one individual who gets incredibly fizzed up on anything in excess of 18 per cent protein, and is ricocheting off the walls on the 22 per cent that her dam manages on quite happily. I had dreadful training problems with the younger bitch until I dropped her protein levels right down, whereupon she became a keen but biddable teammate. No amount of protein will make your dog run any faster than she already can, but it may make her boil over so that she dashes her chances by squandering her energy, tearing needlessly about, and it will certainly stress her kidneys. Too much protein may make your dog lose weight, because she just cannot process it properly. Years ago, I won a bag of very high protein greyhound food in a raffle, and I've never seen my dogs lose condition like it once I started feeding it. Their coats were dull, weight dropped off them and their performance

Kibble food; a popular choice.

dropped right down. There was nothing wrong with the food, but my dogs just could not handle that amount of protein. I gave the rest of the sack away to friends with four lurchers, and these also lost condition dramatically. Personally, I would avoid such stuff even if I were raising purebred sighthounds, because I have seen so much trouble coming from feeding too high.

Apart from convenience, a big plus of commercial food is that the added vitamins and minerals ensure that your dog does not risk going short on essential nutrients. Dry dog food that is fed straight from the sack without soaking will keep teeth in tip-top condition, but if this is how you feed it, ensure that the dog has access to plenty of water, or you'll stress those kidneys again. If you feed soaked food, keep an eye on the state of your dog's teeth, and maybe feed her a handful of dry food daily as well.

Fresh Food

We are always better for eating fresh food, and so are our dogs. Slaughterhouse meat used to be a popular dog food, and there was quite a vogue for green tripe and lights (lung plus windpipe), but this is quite difficult to obtain now, and of course is not so easy to store. Offal and flesh fed raw is good for keeping dogs' teeth clean, but it does sometimes make the dog stink. This may not be a problem if the dog lives in kennels, but is a very different story if she lives in the house with you. Horseflesh especially can strain your relationship with your dog, and the after-effects may need a lot of water and disinfectant to disperse, if yours live in kennels. A diet that is solely flesh, especially muscle meat, is deficient in certain nutrients, notably calcium, which can be remedied by feeding raw meaty bones rather than slabs of pure meat.

Such a diet is the most natural of dog diets. Teeth are marvellous and digestion stays good and strong. You are unlikely to have a dog with anal gland problems if she is allowed to crunch up whole carcases with lots of fur and feather, and despite warnings about bones being dangerous for dogs, raw bones very rarely cause trouble, and when they do, they are usually just stuck across the roof of the mouth, which is easy to remedy. My own vet says that not only has he never had to operate on a dog to relieve impaction in the gut caused by raw bones, he has sent out a general enquiry on the Internet to find if any other vet has come across the problem, with no affirmative replies. Cooking alters the structure of the bone so that it does impact in the gut, with potentially fatal results, but all dogs seem to be able to manage raw bones, which is after all what they were designed to eat. Dogs fed a whole-carcase regime sparkle with health and maintain condition with ease, despite the downside, which is worms. If you do not take suitable precautions, there will be hordes of them.

Many dogs seem to be able to live comfortably with a large worm burden, but it is irresponsible and anti-social to allow this to happen, and ultimately your dog's health will begin to suffer. She will also be sharing her worms with the rest of the world, which isn't really acceptable. However, if you worm her more often than the recommended four times a year, you will be filling her up with strong chemicals which rather negates the effect of feeding a 'natural' diet. You will have people tell you that feeding a rabbit pelt will clear your dog of worms, but I can assure you that it will not. There are good herbal remedies for treating worms, but herbs are strong medicines in their own right, and not to be overused either. In any case, for the kind of worm infestation that your whole-carcase-fed dog is likely to be carrying, you will need chemical wormers.

Nevertheless, if you have access to carcase meat that you are confident is free from worms, for example, of the sort sold

Self-service.

for human consumption, then this is possibly the best way to feed your dog, as long as you ensure that she has free access to grass, herbs and vegetables, which she also needs. It is the way I feed my own dogs most of the time, and I feed flesh that is good enough for human consumption, which does not cause a noticeable increase in the worm burden (though I still worm my dogs four times a year), and nor do the dogs smell offensive. This method does not need to be expensive if you have a kind butcher. I get quantities of boned-out chicken carcases, plus lamb neck and rib-cage, all of which contain sufficient flesh to put weight on the dogs. Chicken drumsticks and wings come on special offer from time to time, as does breast of lamb. This kind of tucker takes time to eat, and really exercises jaws, in fact, if you have smallish lurchers or whippets, it exercises the whole dog, and puppies raised on this sort of food are active and muscular. Teeth and gums become very clean and healthy, dogs that tend to be too lean fill out, and those that have to be dieted, especially spayed or castrated dogs, eat their fill without putting on weight. If you allow this regime, it is important to feed red as well as white meat, perhaps some offal from time to time, and do not trim off fat, for not only is it full of vitamins, but it puts a lovely healthy shine on the coat.

It is absolutely essential to feed fresh fruit and vegetables along with meat. Most dogs will happily crunch up raw vegetables, but the dog's digestion cannot release all the goodness from the cellulose. For best results, raw fruit and vegetables should be put through a liquidizer or a mincer. The resulting mush looks very like the stomach contents that those of us who paunch rabbits or gralloch deer will be familiar with; indeed, it is in this way that wild dogs get much of their vegetable matter. The dog does not need this at every meal, but every other day is a good idea.

Vegetable matter starts to oxidize and lose its goodness very quickly after being cut, so I find the best way is to process a

Tripe, shredded and frozen.

Vegetables for dogs.

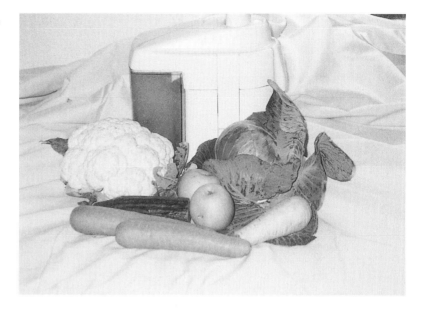

pile of fruit and vegetables once a week, divide into portion sizes and freeze the surplus. It saves me being pinned to the kitchen sink for hours that are better spent out with the dogs, and saves endless washing of domestic appliances. You may have to mix the vegetable slush with meat or add some gravy to get the dogs to take it at first, but you will soon find that they eat it eagerly. A big plus is that dogs so fed no longer need to vomit up bile. Either they do not overproduce it, or the vegetable matter takes it through the stomach to be ejected in a less stressful manner. Sometimes worms are ejected as well, especially in dogs that have not hitherto been fed vegetables. With the exception of potato and onion, all vegetables are suitable for dogs, as are all fruit.

People Food

Table scraps and home-prepared food were all that dogs had in the old days, plus the odd bone from the butcher. I have no bias against table scraps in that if it is good enough for me then it should be good enough for them, but then I eat simple fare. The residue of an elaborate dinner party is unlikely to be suitable for a dog. Dogs love sweets, so do we, but they do neither of us any good, so keep your dog's table scraps to the savoury sort, and be sensible with these. If you prepare fresh food for your dog, what a lucky dog you have! A mixture of raw and cooked meat, raw and cooked vegetables, cooked brown rice, cooked oatmeal, perhaps some plain yoghurt, garlic to repel parasites, chopped cooked nettles and raw herbs for condition, will result in a very healthy dog. Cooked meat should be taken off the bone, for cooked bones splinter and can compact in the gut. Those of us with thieving lurchers know that they seem to be able to survive eating cooked bones very well, but there is no need to go looking for trouble.

Herbage for Dogs

Raw vegetables are a must for dogs, whatever else you feed them. The wild dog can help herself to vegetable matter as she needs to, and also has the contents of herbivore stomachs to eat. Our domestic dogs really do need access to grass, vegetables and herbs. I grow a herb garden especially for the dogs, where they graze at will. Good dog herbs are wild garlic, borage, chives, thyme, parsley, marjoram, sage and rosemary. Couch grass is popular and necessary, and dogs should be allowed to eat their fill of it. It is sometimes known as 'dog grass'. Cleavers (goosegrass) is a favourite with many dogs, especially after the first spring growth, and is known for its cleansing properties. Wheat, oats and barley seem to be very sweet eating in the green stage, but be careful that the crop has not been recently sprayed. Some dogs love raw peas and can do as much damage as pigeons in pea fields, so be farmer-friendly and do not allow your dogs to run riot in someone else's livelihood. A nibble

Cleavers (left) and couch grass.

Vegetables from the previous photo shredded . . .

at the edge of a field can be forgiven, but not wholesale harvesting! Dogs should be allowed fruit as well: all of mine adore fruit and will pick their own if they can. Maize cobs seem to go down very well, often on a pick-your-own basis as when walking by the crop! But again, remember the farmer and don't be a bad neighbour – particularly if you want rabbiting permission later on.

Cooked Food

What of cooked meat and vegetables? Certainly still better then commercial food, if a little less convenient. I always cook rabbits – lurcher owners tend to get a lot of rabbit – and take the flesh off the bone. The worm risk is so high with wild meat that I never feed it raw, but there is no way I am going to waste all those lovely fat rabbits. It used to be thought that feeding a dog raw meat made her vicious, but this is a nonsense, and dogs fed only cooked meat will miss out on some essential nutrients. The same with vegetables: cooked vegetables are better than no vegetables, but some raw meat, some raw vegetables, will make your lurcher a healthier dog. Never feed cooked maize cobs, as these too will compact in the gut, with the potential to kill your dog. If you want to add some cereals, stick with rice and oatmeal; if you want to feed dairy products, I recommend yoghurt only, live and natural not sugary with artificial colouring. A tablespoon of cold-pressed olive or flax oil will be good for the coat and the joints, but if you feed the latter be sure that it is culinary quality and not the stuff you put on your gun stock! Keep away from processed or mixed oils, for heated oils will contain free radicals which are carcinogenic, and mixed oils may contain soya or rapeseed, both of which are bad for dogs. Oils can have a dramatic effect on the digestive system, and are therefore best fed when your dog is able to get out to empty herself. Last thing at night is *not* recommended.

Finally, a word about eggs. Great nutritional arguments rage about eggs, with some people recommending that they are fed daily, while others are convinced that feeding them is detrimental. Both notions are correct, under different circumstances. If your dog has a nutritionally sound diet, then a few eggs are unlikely to do any harm. I have a young dog that is an accomplished egg thief and never seems other than well on it. If the diet is incorrect, don't blame the eggs. Indeed, scrambled eggs are the quickest way I know to settle diarrhoea in a dog. If you feed raw egg, leave the shell for the dog to crunch up as well. Raw egg can make some dogs rather windy, which may be a problem if she lives in the house with you. If you don't like the idea, then there is not a lot to be gained from feeding eggs that cannot be accomplished by feeding other things.

Summary

The very best food for your dog is not always easy or available to every dog owner. I would suggest that, whenever possible, you feed raw meaty bones and raw liquidized fruit and vegetable matter. If, like me, you feed a lot of rabbit and other wild meat, I recommend that it is fed cooked and taken off the bone, though I know a lot of people who do feed unpaunched raw rabbit. The addition of cold-pressed flax or olive oil will add useful nutrients, and plain, wholesome table scraps will be welcomed by the dog and do no harm at all. Personally, I no longer feed commercial dog food, but I recognize that sometimes shortage of time or storage space, or a hiccup in the flesh supply, means that a sack or tin is a useful standby. If that is the case with you, keep an eye on those protein levels, and do not feed anything with added colourants,

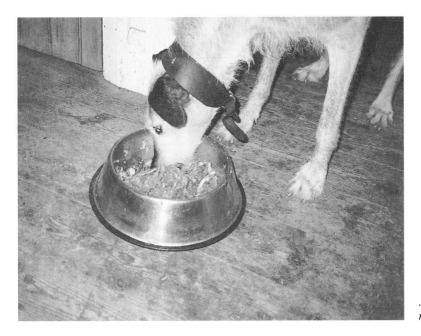

. . . and mixed with raw meat.

molasses, or chemical antioxidants. At time of writing, James Wellbeloved (dry) and Naturediet (wet) are among the best of the manufactured foods. There is a wide choice of manufactured pet food, so before you part with your money, read the list of ingredients carefully.

When to Feed

When you feed a running dog is as important as what. There used to be a curious idea that dogs should fast one day a week, based on the theory that a wild dog would not be able to eat every day. The fasting idea is cheap and convenient for the large kennel owner, but is certainly not suitable for the running dog. This type of dog is all engine, with very little cargo space, and simply cannot hold enough food in one go to maintain condition. If their work schedule allows, they should be fed twice daily. Mine are fed morning and evening unless they are working, in which case they are fed upon their return from work and again eight or so hours later, depending upon whether we are doing day or night work. And here comes another myth that is long overdue for riddance: that the dog must be fed at the same time every day. Interestingly, the strongest exponents of the 'wild dogs don't kill every day' theory are also those who insist that a dog should be fed at exactly the same time on the other six days of the week! In fact, it doesn't matter a jot, and unless you keep staff or are at home all day, you will be pushed to lead a normal life and feed your dogs at the same hour every day – the more so if you are out working one of them. Dogs have a good clock in their heads, and will, if fed to a strict schedule, become agitated as the witching hour approaches.

By all means feed your dogs at the same time if that suits your lifestyle, but don't fret about it if you can't. I have had a lifetime of feeding animals and humans randomly, and I find that as long as enough of the right food is made available at some stage, absence of routine has absolutely no detrimental effect.

Whatever you feed, observe your dog closely; her attitude and condition will soon tell you whether you need to make any alterations. Bear in mind that many longdogs are shy feeders, needing to take their time over their food rather than wolfing it down before the dish hits the floor. If possible, leave the dog alone and in peace to eat, away from other dogs and certainly not in the hubbub of a busy family kitchen. Lurchers are seldom jealous feeders, and my own will cheerfully share their food with each other, often eating out of the same dish or allowing garden birds to hop close and share the scraps. Even the free-range hens have been known to probe their beaks into the dog bowls! So if it is important that each dog gets a specific ration, make sure that they feed alone. You will find it impossible to disguise medication in most lurchers' food – food just isn't that important to them (unless they have stolen it), and if they don't approve of the taste, they will go hungry, for days if necessary. Deerhound crosses, in particular, are very fastidious feeders. If this irritates you, don't get a lurcher with strong sighthound breeding – strong Collie or gundog influence will mean a better eater.

Don't fall into the trap of hand-feeding unless your dog is very ill and needs to be coaxed, for all dogs love to be handfed, and the lurcher, having got you at last where she wants you, will refuse to eat any other way. My own dogs will not eat if I am not present, but then I take bonding to a very

*Raw meaty bones –
lamb spine.*

strong degree. It is a nuisance if I need to go away, though I seldom do, but it does not hurt a dog to go without food for a few days, and it is useful if dogs do not take food from strangers. This is an example of the need that dogs can have for their human companions, and their devotion is not to be taken lightly.

Some breeds of pedigree dog seem to be prone to delicate digestions, often developing a sensitivity even to meat, but this is not usually the case with running dogs, and it is possible that even pedigree dogs would lose their dietary difficulties if they were fed in a more natural way. I have never owned such a troubled dog, so have had no opportunity to experiment.

Water

Before we leave the subject of what goes down a dog's throat, give some thought to drinking water. We all know that dogs must have constant access to fresh, clean water, just as we all know that they seem to prefer drinking out of puddles and filthy, stagnant ponds. Tap water quality varies very much from district to district, and although the water companies assure us that our water supply is the purest and best, the strong smell of added chemicals in some districts makes this difficult to believe. Dogs seem to like fresh rainwater the best, but this is not easy to supply. Filtered water is welcomed by them, and if this seems an unbelievable fuss to you, I suggest that you ask your dog. Put a bowl of filtered water next to a bowl of tap water, and see which one they prefer. Since I started drinking filtered water while living in a district where the supply is heavily chlorinated, I don't see why my dogs should not enjoy the benefits as well. I don't like dogs drinking out of puddles, especially on farmland where all sorts of toxic sprays are used, and drinking out of ponds can cause digestive upsets. Clean running water from streams and rivers should be all right, and you can't wrap the dog in cotton wool; she will have to ingest quite a bit of rubbish in her life, but I do try and avoid manmade chemicals where possible. Wherever you fill your dog's water bowl from, see that she has plenty of it always available, except immediately prior to exertion. Some people like to give their dogs weak sugary tea after a hard series of runs; I don't do it myself, but their dogs enjoy it and it doesn't do any harm.

Exercise – Where, When and How

Exercise is the next cornerstone of fitness. The dog should be exercised and worked on an empty stomach, then fed upon her return at least an hour after she has finished her work. Long, steady walking and trotting harden the feet and tendons. Such exercise is also good for working off any unwanted fat that your dog may have

accumulated before she came into your care. Once she is lean, do not let her put on too much weight again, for a working dog should remain within a few pounds of her ideal weight throughout her life. A bitch that is coming to her season, or having a false pregnancy, will show a weight gain, but this is hormone-induced and should be allowed to happen, just as a suckling bitch must be allowed to eat her fill, but aside from these exceptions, the dog should be kept approximately at her right weight. Excess fat builds up internally before it shows externally, and if she does exert herself with a build-up of fat around her vital organs, the damage that she does may be permanent. Overweight puts extra strain on joints and tendons, again leading to damage. Another old myth is that 'fat turns to muscle' as a dog (or horse, or human) starts to get fit, and so hunters are brought up from summer grazing waddling with obesity, and gone-to-seed boxers puff their way through training for their latest 'comeback' with rolls of fat

Raw meaty bones – chicken carcases.

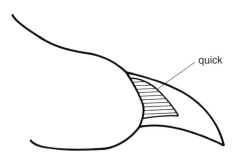

Nail too long.

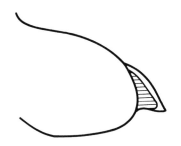

Nail too short.

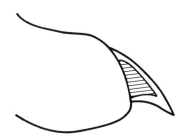

Correct length.

impeding their movement. Fat cells are fat cells, muscle is muscle, and the one cannot transform into the other any more than skin can turn into hair. Start your get-fit programme with a lean dog, increase the feed as you increase the exercise, and you will see her building good muscle without stressing her system.

Once she is at the correct size – it is sufficient to judge by eye at this stage – she can be allowed spells off the lead within her exercise periods, and the road walking can be cut down but not out. There are long muscles with long Latin names that can only be exercised by a dog running free, twisting and turning, pretending to strike at a clump of grass or a molehill and dashing off again. It is very apparent from the musculature alone which dogs are truly worked and which are not. Two dogs together will exercise each other by playing with and chasing each other, but two dogs also make a pack, so you must be on the alert for when they exchange a certain look which means that you are heading for a challenge to your authority. If you have done your recall training properly, you will be able to bring back a solo dog forthwith, but two or more on hot drag can sometimes be a different matter, so it is best to avoid this kind of trouble if you can by constant observation of your dogs – exercising two lurchers together is not a time for woolgathering. When you sense trouble brewing, break up the party by putting one or both on a lead until they have settled down again. If you don't have another dog with which to exercise yours, you will have to find other ways of encouraging her to run. If you have the land available, behind a mountain bike, quad bike or horse is fun, although remember it is illegal to lead your dog on the public road from a bicycle or car.

You would be surprised at how difficult it is to find areas where any dog can run free safely, never mind something that eats distance like a running dog. Parks and beaches can be dog-unfriendly, some banning dogs completely, with others

Sulphur block in water bowl for summer skin irritation.

grudgingly permitting them in restricted areas at certain times only. Public footpaths are legally only rights of access from one place to another; you are not supposed to stray off them and neither is your dog. If she catches quarry while you are at any of these places, you are poaching. In the countryside, everywhere belongs to somebody, and a lot of it is vulnerable: fields of crops or pregnant livestock, pens of gamebirds and the like are no place to have a gambolling longdog running loose. You may have to put in a fair bit of reconnaissance to find places where you can let your dog off the lead to have a good pelt around and blow away the cobwebs. If you have access to a shallow stream or lake with a safe bottom to it, this is another good way

---

Hunting on Horseback

I used to exercise my old dog in her youth by taking her out with my rather flighty Thoroughbred horse. At the time, I had access to a fair bit of private land and bridleway system, with no road work, so it was safe inasmuch as you are never completely safe where animals are concerned. I often used to come home with supper hanging from the saddle, although the horse wasn't overly impressed with having dead bodies close to his person, and I had to lead him home on a number of occasions when he refused point-blank to let me get back on. Hunting on horseback with a lurcher was marvellous fun, although a quiet pony would have been preferable to my regular conveyance. Everybody got really fit, though there was the odd heart-stopping moment, such as when we almost caught a peacock – I'd have had a job hanging that from my saddle. Such outings were sadly missed when the estate was sold and we had to return to conventional exercising.

Dogs must be allowed to eat freely of grass.

of exercising your dog, especially on hot days. Just by walking against the flow of the water, she will be building muscle. Beware of dangerous litter that might cut her feet if you do this, for water has a regrettable effect on some types of human, who suffer from an uncontrollable urge to dump rubbish in it.

When your dog is almost fully fit, you can fine-tune her condition by weight, the way austringers do with birds of prey. Each dog has an optimum working weight,

Good quality rest – (1).

and the handler is the best person to judge this by comparing how she works at different weights. A post-season bitch is often a little heavier, so if she is showing signs of false pregnancy, don't work her hard coursing or lamping, although ferreting and bushing are unlikely to do any harm. During a false pregnancy, certain changes take place within the bitch concerning the distribution of fat around the vital organs. Nine weeks after the season, when she would be giving birth, the hormonal changes in some dogs are so marked that they come into milk, develop nesting behaviour, and grieve for their missing puppies. If this happens to your bitch, she has troubles enough; light work will take her mind off it, but hard work is out of the question, and may even damage her. Some bitches sail through their seasons and never hint at a false pregnancy, but others suffer very much. However, in three weeks or so, when these imaginary puppies would have been weaned, she will be back to her usual sunny self, and can be brought gently back into full work.

Longdogs often do not come into season more than once a year – less is quite common – so it is usually best to let nature takes its course when it comes to false pregnancies. Breeding her does not usually sort the problem, spaying often (but not always) will, but this is a drastic operation that can carry unpleasant side-effects – incontinence is common – and it is best avoided in most cases. Hormone injections to suppress the seasons carry even worse side-effects, and most caring vets no longer recommend these. There is very little problem for the most part with most bitches and their seasons; if you feel that yours is in a situation that for humane reasons (not social convenience) cannot be allowed to continue, weigh up the pros and cons of every option very thoroughly before you finally decide what course of action to take.

Running dogs can lose a lot of weight after a hard working session, and you

Good quality rest –
(2).

will need to compensate for this by careful feeding. If she is the sort that runs up very light, then feed little and often on rest days, which will get more food down her and help to keep the weight on. Some running dogs can look like an anatomy lesson after a prolonged stint of work, and it is your duty to keep your animal looking as reasonable as possible. Lurcher work has quite enough enemies among the ignorant, and although you and I might see a shining coat and eyes, wet nose and beautiful musculature on a dog that is slightly too thin, the animal rights activist who will ignore the genuine cruelty of the grossly overweight, underexercised pet dog, will try to bring the wrath of the authorities down on the owner of the working dog. I have a bitch who burns off weight very quickly, and find that increasing the amount of fatty flesh fed is the only way of covering her bones, but every dog is different and yours might fare better on something else.

Always take good account of the ground over which you run your dog. Deep wet clay will strain her joints and muscles, bone-hard going will give her sore legs and in extreme cases stress fractures, gravel and flinty soils bruise feet and can cause deep cuts. While a working dog must operate on different going, it is folly to take unnecessary risks with her soundness. Keep her nails short, but not too short; the nails act like a footballer's studs when your dog runs and turns, and if yours is the sort of dog that digs out quarry, then she will need something to dig with. Equally, nails that are too long will push up the toe at the wrong angle, resulting in either a broken or a knocked-up toe.

If this should happen, resist all attempts by vets to amputate the afflicted toe, because this puts unacceptable stress on the other toes, changes the angle at which the leg is held, and ultimately damages the hip or shoulder. Any change to the toe arrangements will have a knock-on effect on the rest of the dog, and even a

Good quality rest – (3).

badly broken toe will heal well enough to do much of its original job, which a missing toe cannot. Uneven going is the lot of the lurcher, up and down hills, on and off rocks and walls, and far from the smooth greensward of the Waterloo Cup running grounds. If you get her fit enough first, and rest her properly after each spell of work, she will stand up to any amount of it, but the occasional injury is inevitable, and these will be dealt with more fully in Chapter 6.

Rest and Recuperation

Good quality rest is the last corner of the fitness triangle, and it is surprising how many owners who are fanatical about diet and exercise never give any account to rest. Dogs are designed to sleep for around eighteen hours a day, like other predators. This sleep is light and full of dreams, easily disturbed and easily resumed. Your dog should have a private place of her own in which to sleep, where she is free of disturbance from children, housework, other animals, and the comings and goings of people. She should be warm and dry in her quarters, with a raised bed, so that she does not suffer chill and damp rising from concrete floors. A dog should not be expected to sleep on a blanket on the stone utility room floor, and if she is put to bed cold and wet, then she will obviously suffer ill effects. You would wake up stiff and rheumaticky after such a sleep, and so will she. There are plenty of good dog beds to choose from nowadays; these are money well spent, an investment in the health of your dog.

If your dog's sleeping arrangements are a kennel, shed, boot room or similar, see that her bed is raised off the floor and that she is not interrupted in her rest. If she comes in wet, towel her dry, and be sure that she has plenty of warm bedding. I prefer washable bedding, cornering the

Ex-Battersea dog, breeding unknown, condition perfect.

market in friends' cast-off sheets, blankets, bedspreads and even duvets. There is a product called Vet-bed which is expensive but excellent, wears well, washes easily, is very cosy and wicks moisture away from the dog's body. Remember, a dog that goes to bed wet ends up with wet bedding. Personally, I steer clear of hay and straw, for while both are warm, each harbours fleas, is messy to store and handle, difficult to keep clean and dry, and even more difficult to dispose of. Shavings absorb smells and are easy to clean out, but not very warm. They are unsuitable for unweaned puppies, as bits can be inhaled. Dog bedding must be clean, dry, plentiful and changed often in order to fulfil its function. Do not scorn to put a coat on a dog if the weather is hard; she will sleep that much better for the extra warmth. She is better off wearing a coat in a well-ventilated kennel than shut in without one away from fresh air. A dog which is allowed to become 'thick in the wind' (congested respiratory system) through breathing foul air is never going to run as well as one that has free access to good air.

From time to time, I go rabbiting in the very north of Scotland, staying with friends who are much hardier than I am. The croft is heated by a single peat fire, and one memorable week I slept fully clothed (including coat and hat) in a sleeping bag atop a mattress, with a duvet over all and a lurcher wearing a coat cuddled up on top of the duvet. After a couple of nights, the lurcher came into the sleeping bag with me, and was I ever grateful for her warmth!

If you rest your dog adequately between periods of exercise and work, the faster she will become fit, and she will maintain good condition better. She will also have a longer working life. Peace and quiet, warmth and comfort, will make a hard dog, not a soft one. It is a good regime for us, too.

CHAPTER 5

PERMISSION TO HUNT

Obtaining Your Permission

Unless you already have friends in the farming and fieldsports community, gaining permission to hunt with your lurcher is going to involve a certain amount of homework. It is perfectly possible to be welcomed onto others' land with your running dog, but such permission is not given lightly, and at first you may think that you are never going to make any headway. Don't be discouraged: country people need to be cagey about whom they allow on their land, and most will have had unpleasant experiences with poachers. There are people who use rabbiting as an excuse to have a good look around and see what they can steal, and there are those who are genuine rabbiters but do not show respect for the land. If ferreters leave open holes, if dogs chase stock, if fences are broken and gates left open, this is theft in another form, for it is costing the landowner work and money. Nobody likes hassle: it is easier to say 'no'.

You will hear plenty of 'no' if you go cold-calling. With modern agriculture, it is difficult to find a time when a farmer is not up to his eyes in work, whether farming or paper, and the time of VAT returns is

Rabbit damage in wheat.

particularly hazardous. Similarly with gamekeepers; some of my best hunting permission has come courtesy of gamekeepers, but there are no quiet spells in a keeper's year – just less frantic ones. Gamekeepers meet all sorts of unsavoury types, and take no one on face value. However, they can be extremely helpful to the genuine person who is looking for some work with a well-behaved dog, and they are not as spooky about night work as most people.

If you divide lurcher work in a rough-and-ready manner as bushing, ferreting and lamping, it is ferreting work that you should try for initially. This is because the ferreter is fairly static, as against the lamper, who can cover hundreds of acres in one hit, and landowners can more easily keep their eye on where you are, what you have done, and how you leave the place when you have finished. From your point of view, ferreting is the easiest way in which you can prove that you are doing some good. As you pack up for the day, and

stop to leave a brace of young, paunched rabbits by the farmhouse door, the farmer can see that you have come away with an appreciable number of rabbits. Perhaps on the way to the buries, your dog courses and catches another one or two. Is it all right if you walk round the hedgerows with her before you go, in case any others are sitting out? There is your bushing permission agreed. Presently, you will be able to approach the subject of lamping.

If the farmer allows night shooting, he may well not be happy about you lamping in case there is an accident. Not only is he showing good sense, but the rabbits will already be lamp-shy and therefore difficult to catch. However, a lot of landowners are not in favour of allowing shooting on their land, and in this case will be much more willing to listen to the suggestion that you take your dog out at night. Gamekeepers do so much night work that they are not troubled at all, once they know you, by the thought of lamping. All the better if the keeper wants to come round with you, for

Rabbit damage to maize.

A closer look at that maize.

he can show you the best places and the best lines of approach, while doing his rounds at the same time. Once people know that you and your dogs are reliable, you will be in the happy position of being telephoned with a 'When are you coming over to do something about my rabbits?' or even, 'We've had a fox around again – would you see what you can find?' So how best can you achieve this happy state?

Get to know country people, and give them a chance to get to know you. References are helpful, so are personal introductions, but if you are just getting started, you may not have these at your disposal. But you can buy eggs at the farm-house door, farm produce at the farm shop, chat to the farrier (he will know every-body), the old chap at the allotment, the feed merchant and the village shop. Let it be known that you are looking for a bit of rabbiting, but don't go on about it; presently a bit of chat will come back to you. Go footfollowing the local foxhounds, beagles or minkhounds, go to the point-to-

point, give a hand at the Hunter Trials, and let people see you in a relaxed environ-ment with a common interest. Don't take gossip to heart, but see for yourself how people are; many cultivate an un-approachable exterior, but are lovely people when you get to know them. Game-keepers especially need a local reputation in order to do their job properly, so don't take Old Jeb's 'Adam Perkins won't have a longdog on the place, oh dearie me no' as read. Instead, go to see Adam Perkins, show him your longdog and explain that you won't be any trouble to him, but you may be working local land, so he may see her about. Stress that if the dog is about, so are you, because unaccompanied dogs are a nuisance to everybody, and you don't want him thinking that yours is one of them. When visiting farmer or keeper, arrive in a clean car, be tidily dressed, and don't bring your children. Park consider-ately, leave your dog in the car unless invited to let her out, and if you are and she messes in the yard, as she probably will, clear it up. It is little things that upset people, and this is one of them.

To start with, your permission will be restricted, but just go along with it. Presently, you will be able to extend your remit until you can do pretty well what you like, within the limits of good manners. If you can help out at busy times, so much the better; with or without hunting permission, you will get known, and this can lead to your being allowed to hunt. All sorts of openings can occur: in my own experience as a result of buying hay (for my old horse, but it could have equally well been a guinea pig) and eggs, I acquired a part-time job as a farm secretary, which expanded to helping with free-range poultry, and this led to total freedom to hunt on that farm. Helping out the neighbours at the farmer's request was next; they were 'hobby farmers' with a few rare-breed sheep and fowl, and needed to have some cockerels killed. Not my favourite job, but I did this and stayed to show them how to pluck and draw the birds. I now had

rabbiting permission there as well as the use of the small flock to sheep-train my puppy. You might think that the thirty acres or so of smallholding were not worth bothering with, but these 'hobby farmers' ran a tight ship and sang my praises to another neighbour, who . . . that's how you do it. Don't charge for any help you give, you are just being neighbourly, but you happen to have seen that they have a few rabbits about . . .

Keeping Your Permission

Having obtained your precious permission, be sure to keep it. Let the landowner know when you are coming on the land, and, if possible, when you leave and how you got on. Stop for a chat when you arrive: as well as being polite, it keeps you in touch with what is going on, such as stock being moved, fields to keep out of, can you have a look at that earth in Finches to see if it is active and so on. If you see gates,

Low, slack barbed wire – very dangerous to dogs.

The dog must wait while the field is checked for other hazards.

hedges or fences damaged, or stock in trouble, effect a temporary solution and then tell the farmer straight away – don't wait until you have finished your hunting. A knowledgeable eye round the farm, covering on foot where the farmer has to drive, is worth gold. You will see cartridge cases, though no one has shooting permission, tyre marks, cigarette ends – tell the farmer. At night, you will be an asset to the farm security, coming and going unexpectedly and in silence. "Was that you on my land last night?" I was once asked. "No, I thought not, as you always phone first." It turned out that the local contractor had arranged for a group of his cronies, which included one or two police cadets, to go night shooting without the farmer's permission. This particular farmer did not allow shooting on the farm, and the situation could have been extremely dangerous if I had been out lamping at the same time. With my farm secretary hat on, I was told to write a stiff letter and apologies were duly tendered.

Always tell the landowner that you plan to be on the land; far from compromising your liberty, it is both safe and courteous.

It sometimes happens that the owner of a keepered estate gives you hunting permission, but omits to tell the keeper. Do not let this situation persist: speak to the keeper as soon as possible. He needs to know what you and your dog look like, and he will tell you where you can go and what you can do. His job is difficult enough without finding people on the estate who have been told they can do what they like. You will not be very popular if your dog pins a rabbit by the release pens and forty pheasant poults enthusiastically commit suicide by piling against the opposite side of the fence in a heap. A pheasant's ambition is to die, and the keeper's job (among others) is to thwart it. The keeper knows whether there are wires out, or if he is baiting an area for a fox; in short, he knows which part of his beat can be disturbed and which not. He will be more than pleased for you to thin out the rabbits and,

John Farmer
Clayfields Farm
Heartbreak Hill
Blankshire
10 October 1999

To Whom It May Concern

John Hunter has permission to hunt rabbit, hare and fox on my land by day and night, and to remove the catch.

John Farmer

the van is not to know this. Therefore make it easy for everybody by getting your permission in writing. Farmers hate writing, so you may have to draft out what you want, or even write it yourself on farm headed notepaper for them to sign, but do make that sure you have written proof of your permission. Be very precise in your definition: if you are allowed night hunting, say so, and always state that you are permitted to take your catch away with you. See the example on the left.

When you have your permission in writing, take several photocopies and put the original in a safe place. One of these copies is as good as a reference if you are going to see another landowner about hunting permission, but always ask first if you may do this. If the area that you work is troubled with poachers, it would be as well to lodge a copy of your permission with the police. It is not a legal requirement, nor is telling the police when you are out hunting, but it does save a lot of time and being needlessly stopped. The police

if you are lucky, other things as well, as long as you work with him and not against him. 'Mr Heatons says I can come whenever I want' is not the correct approach.

The same situation applies with the police. You may have hunting permission on hundreds of acres of land, but the copper who stops you in the wee small hours and finds a pile of circumstantial in

*Farm machinery is
a risk to dogs . . .*

. . . and a favourite hiding place for rabbits.

have a job to do, and it is in everybody's interest to prevent poaching. Sadly, we lurcher owners are all tarred with the poaching brush, and poaching is the single biggest threat to the future of lurcher work.

Be very careful that the person who gives you permission is in fact entitled to do so. Farm staff have been known to give permission that the farmer knows nothing about, and the demarcation lines between tenant farmers and their landlords can be blurred in hunting terms. Avoid friction; you are here to catch rabbits, not fire other people's bullets. Sometimes neighbours are less than neighbourly, so always take with caution any statement along the lines of the neighbours not minding if you cross onto their boundary. They generally mind very much indeed. Some of them will come and give you a good screaming at, even if you have not gone onto their land, and I once had a morning's ferreting coloured by a two-acre hobby farmer spitting abuse because his sheep had once been chased by

a lurcher. It is difficult to remain civil in the face of this kind of nonsense, but for goodness' sake do, because the day that you have a go back is bound to be the day that you confront someone who can do you a bad turn and will not hesitate to try. If possible, do not let this kind of bad feeling run, but go to see the person concerned in his own home rather than across a fence (which intensifies territorial aggression, as any dog trainer will tell you), and calmly explain that you have no intention of causing him any trouble, but that you will be working the adjacent land on a regular basis. It is amazing how such people will deflate when approached pleasantly, and after all, they are only going on the attack because they feel threatened and have visions of their homestead being overrun by hundreds of thieving no-goods, with their barn burnt down for a finale.

Most of your hunting permission will be for you only. After a while, you may be allowed to bring a friend, but be very careful who accompanies you. It is not unknown for people who have been taken out as guests to return mob-handed but without you, do damage, and there goes your permission, not just for that stretch of land, but quite possibly for the whole village. Equally, if you go out as someone else's guest, make sure that you really do have permission to accompany them. No one who is hunting legitimately will mind you checking. I used to go out frequently with a friend on a stretch of his permission land that was marvellous for lamping. We used to park in the courtyard and, quiet as we were on the way out, would enjoy a chat on the way back, even as we went past the house and cottages. My friend was generous and took other guests out as well; returning one night, festooned with rabbits, he was stopped by the dairyman. The dairyman, disbelieving that they had permission, went to fetch the landowner, who had consistently refused to give permission in writing. The landowner, who

was very old, was in one of his less lucid spells, and roundly denied having ever set eyes on my friend. I will spare you the rest of the scene, but needless to say it was as well for my friend that his numerous other letters of permission had been lodged with the police. So get it in writing!

Permission comes and goes, land changes hands or changes use, and you may not be welcome where once you were, so always follow up new leads. Sometimes a few acres can lead to a lot more, and a few hours of help here and there can be paid back tenfold. Always be considerate; small issues such as where you park, not slamming car doors or flashing lights near the house can make all the difference. If your working bitch is on heat and the farm dog is male, leave her at home or work elsewhere until she is back to a less exciting state. Equally, if the farm bitch is on heat and your are working a male dog, don't bring him until she has finished. Bitches remain exciting to male dogs for

Fallen trees can hide rabbits as well.

These rabbits were caught by one dog in one morning.

more than a week after the end of their season, so do not be responsible for the farm dog straying or fighting. Do not trust to your own dog's good behaviour and training; the sex drive is extremely strong in some dogs, and it is most unreasonable of you to cause either animal distress, or to be responsible for an unwanted litter of puppies.

When you clear ground for ferreting, remember that everything has to be somewhere, and you will not be popular if the farmer finds rolls of bramble blocking his ditches or left in his arable field. If you cannot get at the rabbit holes without a lot of clearing, say so, and then the farmer will either tell you to go ahead and inform you where to put the debris, or tell you to leave it and try to take the rabbits by other

means. If you are working land next to keepered land, it is a courtesy to check if the gamekeeper would like to be telephoned before you come lamping. Unless you are a landowner yourself, every rabbit that you take is by the grace of someone, and courtesy is always well received. Always turn up when you say you are coming, or let the landowner know at once if you cannot, and don't forget that the catch is the property of the landowner. Most are quite happy for you to keep the bulk of it, or all of it, but never take this for granted. It can take a while to get started with permission land, and you may have to drive long distances or work some unpromising places, but stick with it and I can assure you that you will achieve your hunting permission.

CHAPTER 6

CARE AND MAINTENANCE

Proper care and maintenance will keep your dog working longer and better. After you have invested so much time and work in her, it is folly to cut corners on care. Most working dogs are streets ahead of most pet dogs when it comes to being well looked after – I once (never again) judged a pet dog show full of dearly loved, woefully neglected dogs! But your lurcher needs and deserves the very best of care, and this doesn't take much in the way of time or money, just thoughtfulness.

General Care

When you take your lurcher out working, take a container of fresh water in your car and something clean for her to drink it out of. Puddles and ditches, especially on farmland, can be full of all sorts of chemicals and other filth; don't ever let her drink from puddles near where machinery is maintained, for anti-freeze is sweet to taste, and even a tiny quantity floating on top of a puddle will kill her. Do not let her scavenge food outside, in case she eats a rat full of

Perfect feet from two-year-old dog, lightly worked.

poison, or slug pellets, which will kill her shockingly quickly. If you can, carry either an electrolyte solution, glucose, or (my choice) honey in warm water to give her as soon as her work is over. This will help to restore her if she has exhausted herself, so that she is in good shape to eat and rest as soon as she gets home. Many dogs will not lap this from a bowl, though a little warm, weak tea sometimes helps, and if yours is one of these, then syringe the solution into her mouth before you give her water to drink. Take the chill off the water before you offer it: I carry boiling water in a flask for a variety of purposes, and this is one of them, though care is needed with such hot water. Ice-cold water drunk by a tired, wet dog on a bitterly cold day can upset her stomach or even cause cramps.

First Aid

Carry a simple first-aid kit with you. You need salt (one of those plastic containers for camera films makes a good holder) and another syringe, as large as you can get. Sluicing out a cut with warm salt water will cleanse it and promote clean healing. Take a torch (making sure it works), for injuries that happen at night and for seeing right into a wound. A small pair of sharp scissors is needed for trimming hair away from the edges of a wound, and these should be sterilized before use with boiling water from your flask. Families and scissors have a horrible attraction for each other; if any of your nearest and dearest is likely to 'borrow' these scissors, despite death threats from you, then lock the things away. When you need these scissors, you need them clean and razor sharp, not blunt and covered in goo from cutting out and model-making.

You also require a lot of cheap, tough kitchen paper, gauze bandage, a gamgee pad (cotton wool held in gauze – saddlers sell it) and parcel tape. Parcel tape is vital in a medical kit: cheap, waterproof, tough and easy to apply, it makes bandaging so

Feet of five-year-old dog, hard worked; note swollen centre toe joints and missing nail on outer toe. Despite this, good care ensures that the dog is sound, happy, and continues to work.

much simpler. If the wound is bleeding freely, cleanse with salt water, pad with gamgee, then kitchen paper, and wrap parcel tape around the lot. This will keep things under control until you can get to a vet, and the vet won't have a soggy wound full of bits of muck to pick out before it can be stitched.

An essential aid for a working dog is the homeopathic remedy Arnica, which treats bruising, soft tissue damage and shock resulting from injury or trauma. If your dog has suffered a collision or bad fall, whether there is no visible injury or you fear something really bad has happened, she has much more chance of a rapid and complete recovery, whether subsequently treated by conventional or alternative medicine, a combination of the two, or nothing at all, if she is given Arnica as soon as possible after the accident. In extreme cases it should be given at ten-minute intervals on your way to the vet. Tablet or liquid form is available, but I find liquid easier to give to a dog as it can be dripped straight onto the nose, from where it is licked off.

Remember that it is illegal for a lay person to treat another person's animal for profit. You may legally treat your own dog – you may legally even kill your own dog – provided you do not cause her 'unnecessary suffering'. Most minor injuries can be perfectly well treated by you at home, but if in doubt, or it is something with which you have no experience, then take her to a vet. As in any profession, veterinary skills vary, and not all vets are sympathetic to the concept of working dogs. It is good sense to find your sort of vet before you actually need him or her.

Running dogs are exceptionally sensitive to certain types of anaesthetic; nobody likes to be told how to do their job, but you must ensure that your vet has this fact under consideration if an operation is necessary. The best anaesthetic for gazehounds is also the most expensive, and for this reason is not routinely made available, so do make it clear that the cost does not matter – it is not devastatingly expensive, and may be the difference between a dog that will be working again and one that will not. I have seen lurchers recover from the most appalling accidents, indeed, I had to fast-talk one heartbroken man out of shooting his dog on the spot not long ago, but every minute counts in getting her to a vet after a really bad mishap. Incidentally, this dog made a full recovery and is now working again.

For everyday cuts, it is sufficient to cleanse the wound with salt water, and then leave it to fresh air and licking. Do not use iodine, as this is extremely toxic, and if you must use disinfectant, use the stuff that is considered safe for babies, and only use it once. A very few dogs will worry at an injury and make it worse; most will lick just enough to keep it clean and comfortable. If yours is the sort to niggle at a wound, don't use the 'lampshade' type collars to stop her reaching round, as most sighthounds panic themselves into a frenzy with these. It is possible to get a wide, thick collar that fits the whole of the neck and is much less stressful for the dog. They are quite easy to make if your vet cannot supply one.

Deep wounds, and those that need poulticing, can also be cared for quite easily. Trim the hair from around the wound and then syringe it out thoroughly with salt water. Smear a generous glob of solid honey – unblended organic is best, but ordinary will do – onto a double folded sheet of kitchen paper, and arrange it over the injury so that the honey is exactly

Feet of twelve-year-old dog, worked too young. Tendons slack, toes spread.

over and in the hole. Tape over with parcel tape. Such a poultice will pull the most amazing muck out of a wound – I have treated deep, suppurating holes that have cleansed and healed beautifully, but you and I would never let an injury get to that sort of state. A poultice is only effective for half an hour to an hour, after which it should be removed and changed for a fresh one if the wound is still dirty, or the injury left to fresh air if it has cleansed. I use a poultice twice a day for the first day if the injury is fresh and has not been neglected, then once a day for the next two days, after which it should be judged by eye. A clean wound is pink and sweet-smelling, and do not panic about colourless or light yellow sticky fluid forming, for this is part of the healing process. If, however, the wound stinks, and is full of dark yellow or greenish matter, this is *wrong*, and your dog needs help in a hurry. You do not want a deep wound to crust over; it has to be kept open and heal from the inside out. Poulticing and dog licking is a good way of making this happen. There is a tendency to leave poultices on for too long, which kills the skin at the edge of the wound. Put it on, let it do its stuff, then take it off. I have treated some awful injuries on animals and people with the honey poultice method, and never had any other result but a clean wound that healed very fast. Other poultices that have been used with great success involve cooked onion and/or garlic bound into brown bread or oatmeal, and wrapped in a muslin before application, but frankly, I have never found anything better than honey, so always keep some in your larder.

If you are dealing with the kind of wound that must be covered over, such as a split pad, then a thick wad of kitchen paper under the paw, covered with a sock from one of those strays that you never find the partner to, and then the sock taped at the top, will be enough for dry conditions. For the wet, a thick layer of parcel tape or a plastic bag taped over will last long enough for the dog to go out and empty herself, but remove waterproofing afterwards, as the heat and condensation that it generates will be detrimental to the healing process. A baby's disposable nappy can be a useful wound pad as well. There are some natty 'boots' that can be bought to fit over a dog's paw and leg, and it is worth investing in one of these, but again, these should be removed as soon as possible because of the waterproofing.

Feeding During Convalescence

If your dog is laid up with injury, cut her protein levels right back for the duration. She needs good food to help her to heal, but she does not need high protein. It will put her system, particularly her kidneys, under strain at a time when it is already under duress, and it won't do much for you trying to keep her quiet when she is

desperate to burn off some energy. Feed plenty of vegetables and fruit at this time, and if you are cooking for her, add cleansing herbs such as nettles, cleavers and parsley. Make sure that she has lots of fresh water, for she may need to drink quite a bit more than usual while she is healing.

Antibiotics

Antibiotics are lifesavers, but bodies very quickly build up an intolerance to them. There may come a time in your dog's career when antibiotics are essential, and they will be more effective if she has not had repeated doses of them previously. A simple wound kept clean does not need antibiotics – you would not use them on yourself for such an injury, and your immune system is far weaker than your dog's. As long as she is in good general health, she will recover very quickly from wounds.

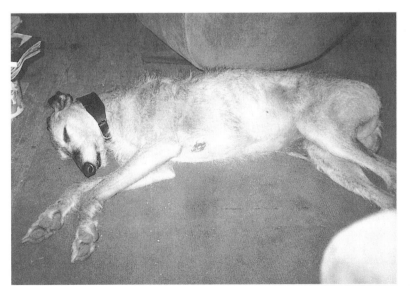

Barbed wire injury.

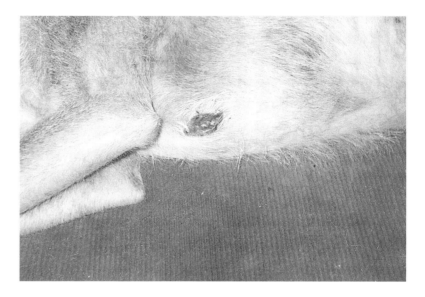

Same injury close up; kept clean and left open, it healed perfectly.

Soft Tissue Injuries

Sprains and strains are a regular part of an athlete's life, and that includes running dogs. Just like a human athlete, you can minimize the chance of injury by warming her up before she works and warming her down afterwards. It is folly to unload a dog from a van and work her straight away. With most lurcher disciplines, the trot from vehicle to field will be enough to loosen her up and warm her muscles, but if you expect her to be running hard, she will appreciate a warming rub down. Coursing enthusiasts use their own favoured liniments and embrocations, though I would suggest that this is giving too hard a task to your dog if you then expect her to use her nose! By all means rub her down with embrocation when her work is finished; she will enjoy it and it will do her good.

Before starting work, give your dog a quick massage, using a lightish pressure and covering the fleshy parts of neck, shoulders, back and quarters with circling movements of your fingertips. Then sweep your hands down the length of her neck and back and give her tail a gentle stretch. We who do not have tails tend to underrate their importance. Afterwards, she will shake herself like a falcon rousing and be ready to go. Upon return from work, do the same again, and let the sensitivity in your fingertips alert you to thorns, swellings and any area where she does not like being touched. Put a coat on her if it is cold, towel her off if she is wet, and if you have a long journey home, again, put a coat on her. Cold muscles can go into spasm; cold muscles that have been stressed can even tear. A chilled, soaking-wet dog that has been rubbed down and coated will be relaxed, warm and dry by the time you get her home. She will be more likely to eat all her supper and go straight off to sleep, which means that when you want her to work the next day she will be fully rested and ready to go. A dog that does not have this consideration is much more likely to pull out stiff and tired next time, and you will be laying the foundations for a slow recovery rate and maybe even arthritis.

Assuming there are no injuries that require your attention, get some electrolyte or similar down your dog, and then offer her a drink. While she is drinking, check over her feet, especially toes and nails. Then take her home, give her a snack of something light and digestible, and leave her to rest. A tired dog will not welcome grooming or a heavy meal, but when she has had her main sleep, take her out to empty herself, being aware of how she is moving. A little stiffness that soon wears off is not important, but lameness is. Check her over thoroughly, feed her a main meal, and then leave her to rest again.

If there is heat or swelling in any area, she needs to be checked by an expert. Strains that are treated and rested as soon as they appear will get better much more quickly; if a dog is worked while she is 'pottery' the injury can only get worse – often considerably worse. Some people are very anxious to get a swelling down, which is easy enough with an ice pack, but it is worth remembering that swelling exists to protect the site of an injury while it heals. An injury that has had the swelling artificially reduced *has not healed*. Pain exists to stop the injured area being damaged with further use – pain reduced by drugs *has not healed*. Get the injury diagnosed, and then use good old Doctor Time. Rest is a grand healer of strains and sprains, and a good physiotherapist will show you how to massage above the site of such an injury in order to increase blood flow to the affected area and promote healing. There are a variety of electrical therapies, such as laser, ultrasound and so on, which are widely used to accelerate healing, but they should only be used by qualified prac-

titioners. I am qualified in the use of these myself, but I find that my hands are infinitely more sensitive and so prefer to use those.

Bones

Dislocations and fractures need fast treatment, but the recovery rate is good. A limb coming out of plaster can look horrific, wizened and twisted, with the fracture site swollen and distorted, but don't worry, it will fill out and straighten in the majority of cases. Massage above the plaster will make all the difference to the blood flow of the affected leg, and five minutes several times a day is much more beneficial than twenty minutes once. I treated one of my dogs after a nasty break in three of the four long bones below the hock (metatarsals), and the affected leg was the same size as the other one when the plaster came off. A broken leg may be a year in straightening, though your dog will run sound on it much sooner. Be patient, don't overuse her, and while she will never be quite as good as new, she will certainly be able to work almost as well.

Dislocations that are attended to quickly should recover without leaving a sustained weakness of the joint. Initially, because tendons have been stretched, the injury should be treated as a fracture, with rest and confinement followed by lead exercise for six weeks or so. The homeopathic remedies Arnica and Ruta Graveolens used together are excellent for healing the damage associated with dislocation – give initially four times daily, cutting down to twice daily after the first week and once daily after the second week, or as directed by your vet. As a result of a lamping accident, one of my dogs sustained such a severe dislocation that both the vet and I suspected a multiple fracture. While under anaesthetic for the X-ray, the limb was pulled in such a manner that it relocated. Within two days, the dog was walking sound, and, after the treatment described, returned to work none the worse in eight weeks. It didn't do a lot for my nerves, though!

The Arnica and Ruta mixture also proved to be a great help to another of my dogs which sustained a cruciate ligament injury. This ligament holds the stifle joint secure, and it is not the sort of injury from which running dogs make a complete recovery. In circumstances like this, one faces a lonely and difficult decision based on what sort of quality of life can be offered to the dog thereafter. The vet decided not to operate except as a last resort, and we treated the injury homeopathically as described. It was a long business, but the bitch, who is exceptionally dear to me, is certainly enjoying her retirement, and though she will never work again,

can run well enough to play mad lurcher games.

Over-Running

Many lurchers have no 'safety stop', that is, they will just keep going, and can literally run themselves to death. It is exactly the same kind of spirit that has caused Thoroughbred racehorses to run on to the end of a race with a fractured leg. Therefore, you must stop working your dog each time before she is overused, and if she has a collision or seems to lose her rhythm when running, stop her right there and take her home. 'One-more-rabbititis' is a common disease in lurcherfolk, but no rabbit is worth a permanently damaged dog. Accidents do happen, and dogs will over-run through no fault of their handler. If this does occur, then she has priority over everything, so get some fluids down her, take her home, keep her warm and rested, and don't work her again for a few

Cooling off.

days. She will tell you when she is ready to go again by skittish behaviour when out on exercise, but if she is unnaturally calm and just wants to eat and sleep, let her. It is the damage you can't see, to heart and lungs, liver and kidneys, that needs this time to repair. If the dog is repeatedly overused, then the organs will lose their ability to mend, and the dog is then referred to as 'blown'. A dog that has over-run will be reluctant to eat and will sleep like the dead for hours. During this time, her body temperature may drop dramatically, so keep her warm, using a coat or even a heat lamp if necessary. I remember reading an old gamekeeper's memoirs, from the days when people and dogs were literally worked until they dropped. He stated that dogs were not to be left curled up outside after work because they would be found curled up dead the next day! Cold is a swift, silent killer to a tired dog; exposure to it does not toughen a dog up, nor does warmth make a softie of her, so

please take as much care of her resting accommodation as you do over her food.

Exercise in Pregnancy

Bitches need extra consideration during false pregnancy, and even more during a real one. It is best not to work a pregnant bitch at all, though she will need her usual exercise, and although most running dogs show little sign of pregnancy until the sixth week, the embryos are vulnerable and so is the bitch. As she swells during the last week of her pregnancy, her system will be working flat out to carry away both her waste products and the pups', so no additional strain should be put on her. Equally, after the birth, while she is suckling and cleansing, do not work her. When the pups are weaned, and when she is no longer showing any discharge from the vulva (which is normal and can go on for some weeks), she can be brought back gently into fitness. Don't rush her; just exercise

Basic first-aid kit.

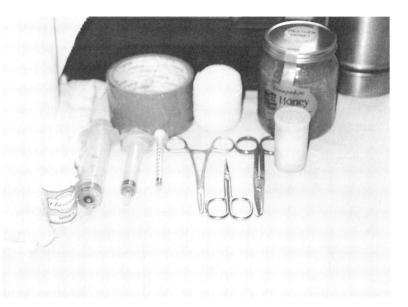

L to R back: kitchen paper, parcel tape, crêpe bandage, honey, flask of hot water.
L to R front: Arnica tablets, three sizes of syringe, forceps, curved scissors, round-ended scissors, container of salt.

her carefully until she gets her figure back. Birth may be a natural process, but so is death, and if you think that this has been a restful time for her, ask the Missus!

Itchy Things

Keep on top of the parasites that are the inevitable result of letting a dog step outside, and keep bedding clean as well. A daily flea-combing in the season will keep all but the heaviest infestations at bay, and if you dip the flea comb into water that has had a few drops of Lavender Oil added, this will help to repel fleas, ticks and other small bloodsuckers. If the flea situation does get out of control, the safest product currently available is 'Frontline', which is also effective against mange. Treat with caution any product that requires either the wearing of protective clothing when you apply it to your dog (some of the more alarming products insist that you do not touch your dog or sleep in the same room as her after the application of their 'safe' chemical), or products that require the flea to bite your dog to ingest the chemical which is now in its bloodstream. Working dogs are constantly in contact with a wide range of fleas, so you need something which kills or repels the flea before it bites. Fleas also spread tapeworm, so use a wormer that will deal with these after you have had a flea infestation. Drontal Plus is good and as safe as any.

Ticks are more straightforward to deal with in that they breathe through their abdomens, so any substance that seals the abdomen suffocates the tick, such as butter, nail varnish or typewriting correction fluid (in my household this is used a lot, being referred to as 'Tick-Ex'). Or you can use irritants such as surgical spirit or aftershave lotion, which will weaken the tick or may even make it back out. For some reason, they are easier to extract if you give them a half-turn anticlockwise. I

Packed and ready to go.

often read that disaster will befall the animal whose owner only partially extracts the tick, leaving the head and mouthparts under the skin. This is nonsense. If you accidentally do this, the affected area will form a scab which will carry the tick remains out with it in a few days. Nature is not so ineffective as not to cope with such a common situation. If, however, you are concerned, dab the area, which will be slightly raised like a gnat bite, with salt water or a dog-friendly disinfectant. Ticks do carry Lyme disease, which has flu-like symptoms and can affect us as well, so if you or your dog become off-colour during tick season, seek appropriate medical help. The chances are that your vet will know more about it than your GP unless you live in a country area.

If your dogs are kennelled, then a twice-yearly deep cleansing of the kennels and runs will be needed to get rid of parasite eggs and larvae. If the dogs live in the house with you, invest in a really powerful vacuum cleaner.

When it comes to keeping your dog in fine fettle, it is the eyes and hands of the Master which will provide the best tools. You will need to become sensitive to every little change in bearing and temperament. Some lurchers can be amazingly stoical about discomfort, so if a good worker starts to 'jack', refuse to work or start pulling up on her rabbits, always look for a physical cause first. As far as your working excursions go, plan for the worst and hope for the best, and you will just about have it right.

CHAPTER 7

LOST, STOLEN OR STRAYED?

It is a moment of pure, gut-wrenching horror. You get home and your house or kennels have been broken into. Your dogs have gone. In a matter of hours, they could be several hundred miles away, sold on or used and dumped. Every year, hundreds of lurchers, terriers and gundogs, but particularly lurchers, 'disappear' from cars, outside shops and from their own homes. Dogs being exercised run out of sight and never come back. It has happened to me, and there is no grief like it.

Why do people steal lurchers, which are not expensive to buy? There is a thriving second-hand market for these lovely dogs and, although they often change hands for ludicrously low sums of money, it is a way for the unscrupulous to get hold of dogs that are 'ready to go', without the bother of raising or training them. Often, bitches are stolen for breeding, and then dumped once the pick of the litter has been taken. Sometimes a dog is stolen and used at stud, being dumped, if it is lucky, after the required service. Most often, dogs are taken to be used in illegal gambling matches, after which the people concerned – who are almost always travellers – just drive off and leave them. Sometimes the dogs go for medical research, the tremendous good health of the average lurcher being an asset in this industry. Very occasionally, the dog will be bought in good faith by someone who gives it a decent home, but for the most part, if your running dog is stolen, the purpose of the theft will not have been to her benefit, and you are going to have to move very quickly in order to get her back.

Tracking Down Your Dog

In the working dog world particularly, trouble does not cease if the animal is found by someone. As a very nice policeman said to me, "It might be your dog, love, but in law it is just a chattel." The police have worse crimes to deal with than what, to them, is a simple theft of property. All that they are required to do is note down the details – it is up to you to find your dog, and time will not be on your side.

The dog picked up by a member of the public and taken to the police has seven days of life left. First it is sent to the local authority dog pound. By law, these dogs should be kept for seven days, but there are some 'rescue' centres that have a policy of killing working dogs as soon as they come in. The official line is that they are impossible to rehome, but in fact this is an animal rights' agenda, dreamed up by those who object to dogs being used for hunting.

Dogs taken to the National Canine Defence League (NCDL), the RSPCA and private animal sanctuaries sometimes fare better, although only the NCDL and the Blue Cross have a policy of not executing healthy dogs. Sadly, very few organizations make even a token effort at tracing the dog's owner. It is a legal requirement for your dog to wear a collar with a tag that carries your name and address. A reflection on the age of this law is that a telephone number is not mandatory, though most of us will include one. But a dog thief is not going to leave a collar and ID on the dog. That leaves you with the back-up of tattooing or microchipping, both of which have their disadvantages. Tattoos can blur and become unreadable; if on an ear, it has not been unknown for the ear to be cut off, and if on the inside of a hindleg, how many people are going to check that on an unknown dog, even if they think that it might be there?

The microchip also has drawbacks: many people are reluctant to introduce a foreign body under their dog's skin, as the chip has been known to migrate in a significant minority of cases. Nor do all Dog Rescue centres have the scanner that will read the chip. Of those that do, not all of them routinely use it, or think to check the whole dog in case the chip has migrated. A friend's microchipped terrier went missing, and was picked up by a member of the public and taken to a local authority

Never leave your dogs outside a shop.

kennels. The terrier was not scanned because he was not wearing a collar with the tag to state that he had been microchipped! There is always a fool bigger than a foolproof system. However, if your dog has nothing, she has far less chance of ever seeing you again, and proper ID, tattooing and/or microchip may just tip the balance in favour of your dog's return home.

The NCDL issues a useful 'Lost Dog' pack, which advises you which authorities to contact and the importance of continuing to call them. 'Centralization' means that a lot of messages do not get passed on to the right quarters (our local policeman found a friend's dog, and because he recognized it, was able to return it, but the central information office had not circulated the dog's description at all), and I discovered to my cost that with police and Dog Rescues alike, details are not passed on from shift to shift, but are simply lost with a turn of the page on which they are written. Others have no idea of dog descriptions ("What is brindle?"), so that if your lost dog was in front of them as they took the call, they would not make the association. Large organizations such as the RSPCA may well move a dog out of the area if the local kennels are full, so that while you are tearing one county apart trying to trace your dog, she is in fact in another.

The dog has a unique and unpleasant position in law in that if it is picked up supposedly straying it becomes the property of the local authority. If it is then rehomed, it becomes the property of

The National Strays Bureau and 'Lurchersearch UK'

There are now the beginnings of several central information offices available to assist in tracking down lost or stolen dogs.

The National Strays Bureau (NSB) can be contacted on 0897-123-999, where for a one-off charge of £7.50 plus the cost of the call at £1.50 per minute (at the time of writing), they will check their database for you for four weeks. If you have found a dog, the number to call is 0990-168-220. All the police, animal sanctuaries and dog rescues large and small need to do is report their 'found' dogs on this number. I spoke with Marek Kirwald at the NSB head office and he informed me that, after piloting the scheme in the London area, it has been extended countrywide. Authorities in most areas have been quick to realize the advantages of using this service, especially where the police have been actively leading the way. However sophisti-cated the software (and I am assured that it is, very), the stumbling block is always the liveware, so here's hoping that those authorities who are being a little slow to catch on become more co-operative. The Bureau also offers a life registration service for dogs and cats, which includes a collar tag and free use of the lost and found service. Details from The National Strays Bureau, Thornton House, Thornton Road, Wimbledon, London SW19 4NG.

Specifically for lurchers, we have the organization 'Lurchersearch UK' run by people who really understand the scale of lurcher theft and the type of people that we lurcher owners are up against. There are co-ordinators in each area, and an extremely fast and efficient network of contacts. Initial calls should be to Judy on 01743-821623 or Barry on 01598-753563.

the new owner. It can be microchipped, tattooed, registered and scream with joy upon seeing you, but legally it is no longer your dog. Even a camera has more status. A stolen horse, if resold, is still the property of the original owner, who can claim it back, but your stolen dog can be re-homed by an organization that has made not the slightest effort to trace you, and if the new owners are not decent people, you will have to take them – not the animal organization – to court.

As well as repeatedly telephoning and visiting every dog rescue that you can find, you should flood the area with posters and leaflets bearing a description and preferably a photograph of your dog. Lots of them will be taken down as soon as you put them up, so you will need plenty. That is how I got my dogs back, with the help of a good friend who had a photocopier and boundless energy. There was a leaflet through every door, and a poster at every car park and popular dog-walking area, and on many lampposts as well. If you do this, please have the courtesy to take the posters down after they are no longer needed, and likewise tell the police and dog rescues that you have found your dog. I was very fortunate to get my dogs back, and it was the slenderest thread of coincidence that did it, even though they had full ID. Interestingly, I was getting telephone calls of sightings of my dogs some two weeks after I got them back, which may have been something to do with the mention of a large reward for 'information leading to their safe recovery'. As well as posters, try and get both the local and the sporting press interested, as many of them run 'missing dog' advertisements for free, and you have nothing to lose by trying local radio or even television. Your dog might be on a boat to Ireland – the way a lot of them go – within hours, but it is possible to make her well enough known that you get her back. Take any chance you can, because there are not so many chances with a lost dog.

Protecting Your Dog

It seems a great pity that the popular dog magazines and the multitudes of 'Rescue' associations, from the very largest to the very small, neither alert dog owners to the dangers of having their pets stolen, nor give publicity and assistance to the organizations that strive to return our dogs to us. There are precautions that you can take to protect your dog from theft, and though they sound obvious, it is worth running through them. Never leave your dog outside a shop or pub, even for a couple of minutes. Never leave your dog alone in the car. If you go to a dog show which does not offer ringside parking, turn the car around and leave the showground, pausing only to tell the organizers why. A lot of dogs get stolen at dog shows. Do not leave your dog in the charge of a child: dogs have been taken out of children's hands with a comment like "Your Dad said I was to take him over there", leaving the child weeping and the dog lost. If you win a trophy and the club wants your name and address (they like to get their trophies back at the end of the year!), stress that this must be kept confidential – winning dogs are traced to their homes and stolen in this way. If you drive away from an event and have reason to believe that a vehicle is following you, don't show its occupants the way to your home! If you breed a litter of lurcher pups, be very careful about the people who come to your home to see them – it is quite

*Leaflet from
Lurchersearch UK.*

LURCHER

HAS YOUR DOG BEEN STOLEN OR LOST?

ENLIST THE HELP OF

LURCHER *Search* U.K.

We may be able to help you. By reporting to us the loss of your dog or any suspicious vehicle or incidents immediately, we can set in motion our telephone network of people nationwide including Ireland. Within hours these people will be looking out for your dog or making other people aware. We are in contact with dog wardens, rescue centres and police.

JUDY: 01743 821623

BARRY: 01598 753563

BY JOINING OUR NETWORK YOU CAN HELP US TO STAMP OUT DOG THEFT!

SEARCH

WE CAN DO THIS WITH YOUR HELP!

common for bitch and pups to be stolen not long after strangers have been to see them. If possible, use a different address or a friend as a go-between.

If you are tempted to think that all of the above is a bit fanciful, ask around, and you will be shocked at the number of people to whom it has happened. I was once caught in a traffic jam when a travellers' pickup drew up alongside me and an attempt was made to take my dogs from the back of my car. If I had not locked them in, as I do routinely, there is no doubt that I would have lost them. In a nutshell, never, ever leave your dog unattended, and don't boast to strangers about how good she is. Anyone who is determined to steal a dog will steal her, and any kennel or house can be broken into, given time, so see to it that your brand of security does not allow thieves time. If you use a guard dog – and plenty find them the best of all deterrents – remember that a dog will always be distracted by a bitch, but a bitch will not be distracted by a dog unless she is on heat. A guard bitch is therefore a better proposition, because dog thieves know dogs and will take your guard dog as well if they dare. Dog theft is a most despicable crime, and is carried out by some very nasty people.

It has always bothered me that Dog Rescues large and small spend so much time, effort and money rehoming 'strays' that already have loving homes, while distraught owners are combing the district for them, when it would be so much easier and cheaper to go all out to find the owners and save the new homes for dogs that genuinely need them. Now, all these worthy authorities have access to Lurchersearch UK and the National Strays Bureau, where they just have to make one call to each, and all the rest is done for them. We working dog owners, who know just how big the dog theft problem is, should give these organizations all our support. I hope you never need them. I hope I don't either. But make a note of the numbers – please – now.

CHAPTER 8

BREEDING YOUR OWN

Why Breed?

If you were to ask me whether you should breed your lurcher, I would recommend that you did not. You would then be entirely justified in reminding me that I breed my own replacements. There are many pitfalls to lurcher breeding, and yet I still breed my own. This chapter will outline the few benefits and the many problems associated with lurcher breeding, after which you will be better able to decide whether you really want to go through with it.

Why breed, when the Dog Rescues are full of unwanted, discarded lurchers? Perhaps you have had so much pleasure from your dog that you would like your next one to be as much like her as possible. Perhaps, now that she is old, or injury has ended her working life, you would like her to have a litter to occupy her. Perhaps you know breeders of pedigree dogs, who seem to make a tidy profit from each litter, and you feel that your bitch can earn you some money in the summer by doing the same? If the latter is the case, I can assure you that all you will make, even if all goes well, will be a thundering loss. A pup bred for your own use will work out as the most expensive pup that you will ever have. The only way to make money out of breeding lurchers is either to have a big commercial kennel (and remember that there are several of these already serving a small market of would-be lurcher owners), or to not 'do' the bitch and pups properly. If you skimp on their welfare, you will not only raise rubbish, but you will damage your bitch. Raising a litter is not just a matter of leaving bitch and pups in a kennel or shed and adding food and water at intervals. Done properly, it is an expensive and time-consuming process. It is also, I have to say, so very rewarding that every few years, I breed another litter when I need a new lurcher. Read on, and see if I can put you off doing the same.

Choosing a Mate

Because lurchers are mongrels, breeding them involves science and art. The science is that of genetics, but the art is part intuition and part luck. The more different breeds that are combined in dog and bitch, the more varied is the litter that results. This is not automatically a bad thing, for you will only be keeping one pup and you will have to find homes for the others, and not everybody who comes to look at your litter will be after exactly the same sort of animal. If you breed, say, a Collie/Greyhound to a Greyhound, the results will be predictable. If, however, you breed a good working lurcher to another good working lurcher, you may safely say that you will get a litter of good working lurchers, but they are likely to be very different in size, colour, coat, temperament and proportions. If you have, on both sides, stock with the potential for inherited health problems, you may have unwittingly bred a canine time bomb. For example, some purebred Bedlingtons carry copper toxicosis, some purebred Deerhounds carry liver shunt, some purebred Border Collies carry a plethora of inherited eye and hip diseases. If each parent carries recessive genes of the same disease, there is a strong possibility that some of the pups will be affected.

Temperament is also important. A dog with a suspect temperament should not be bred from, no matter how good a worker. Soundness is of relatively little account: many excellent working lurchers retire early due to accidents, and it is sometimes said that the best ones are the ones that injure themselves, because they try their hardest, whereas the cowardly dog that does not give its all will not hurt itself. So, do not reject a dog for breeding because it has been injured. Conformation should, however, be a matter of importance, not only because dogs that are made right move right, but because an attractive dog has a better chance in life than an unattractive one. If your own dog has physical attributes or working skills which could be improved, then choose a mate that offers what is lacking. For instance, if yours is a reluctant retriever, pick a natural retriever; if she is light in the quarters, find a dog that is strong in the back end. Above all, remember that your pups contain not just the genes of their parents, but the genes of all the generations that have gone before. Breeding pedigree dogs is enough of a gamble; breeding lurchers can be full of surprises. And some of those surprises can be very nice indeed.

If you mate a large and a small dog together, you will not get pups that level out evenly between the two sizes. You will get large pups, small pups and medium pups. Assuming good rearing, the small pups will mature into smaller dogs than the medium and large, which will remain medium and large. For instance, I mated a 26in (66cm) bitch (Deerhound/Greyhound/Whippet) to a 19in (48cm) dog (Bedlington/Whippet) and kept a smallish dog pup which matured at 22in (56cm). Other dog pups matured at their dam's height; had there been any small bitches, they would have ended up smaller than the dog that I kept. If, however, any of those pups are bred from, they contain very large Deerhound genes, Greyhound genes, as well as small Whippet and Bedlington genes. Put to a small lurcher, there is still the potential for a 'whopper', but if you put to a large one, there could yet be a small-is-beautiful pup or two that might be considered 'runts' but in fact would be anything but. So when you choose the size of stud to put to your bitch, be aware that if there are differing sizes in the backgrounds of the parents, then so will your pups differ. In purely physical terms of mating, it is kinder to put a same size or smaller stud dog over your bitch, especially if she is a maiden bitch. The act of being mated by a bigger dog is sometimes very distressing for the bitch, possibly causing her to become difficult to mate on future occasions. It is veterinary opinion that the bitch dictates the size of the pups, but my own experience indicates that you often get one huge pup in the litter, which can give the bitch birthing difficulties.

Take a dispassionate look at your bitch. If you would like a pup exactly the same, choose a stud dog that is as much like her as possible. If you would like more coat, better feet, stronger quarters and so on, choose a stud who has these attributes. If you know the dog and have seen him work, so much the better. If both parents do the job that you want done, then the pups should also do that job. For instance, I wanted my 22in (56cm) dog as a rabbit catcher, which he certainly is, but he comes from four generations (possibly more) of foxing dogs, and self-entered to fox very early. Fox is the quarry he wants above all others, and all his littermates are the same. Tractability can be bred in (or out), as can the tendency to hard mouth.

You must decide what matters most to you, based on the country and quarry that you work, and then choose the mate for your dog accordingly. What about age? The best age in health terms to breed a bitch is from two to four, but this is counterbalanced by the fact that you do not have the true picture of her worth at two, whereas at four she will be in her absolute prime, and so it is downright

wasteful to take her off work for so long at this time. A first litter should not be bred from a bitch much older than five without expecting some complications. However, there are some running dog breeds in India which are so tough that bitches are not bred from at all until they are eight years old, when, like racehorses, they are retired to stud. This is because the Indian environment is so harsh that natural selection rules that only the very strongest dogs last long enough to breed. Do not breed from a very young bitch: this is downright cruelty. To subject her to the stresses of pregnancy when she is not fully developed in herself will weaken her beyond repair. If yours is the sort that only comes into season every few years, you will not have much choice in when to breed her.

With a male dog, it is much easier to choose when to breed. I once used a yearling male on one of my bitches. He was barely entered to quarry, but he was biddable, well bred and well proportioned. It was his first service and the pups were

Deerhound / Greyhound pup, seven months; a gangly pup named Ralph who shows great promise.

crackers. Using an elderly dog, the drawback is that the sperm will not be so lively, and it is possible that some of the pups will be dead or malformed. This is of little account with a healthy young bitch, but may lead to a smaller viable litter in an old bitch. Still, how many pups do you need? The most important issue is that dog and bitch are healthy. If you are putting a bitch in whelp because she has been sidelined through injury, please give thought to the weight of the pregnancy and even to the vigour of the mating, and be sure that she is capable of withstanding these events.

The Mating

Whereas most dogs come into season at six-monthly intervals, lurcher bitches, especially those with a lot of sighthound in them, may only come in once a year, like wolves and other wild canids. Some are very erratic with their seasons, and many will go years without coming on heat, though once they have bred, most will settle to an annual cycle. Equally, male gazehounds often have a low sex drive, which makes them pleasant to live with and easy to keep entire, but brings its own problems when you want to arrange a mating. Stud dogs used commercially will obviously be more experienced and more obliging, though even they can need some coaxing. However, the privately-owned dog that has perhaps been actively discouraged from mating in the past will need tact and time. There are always exceptions to this, and the accidental and unwanted mating is always the one that takes place quickly,

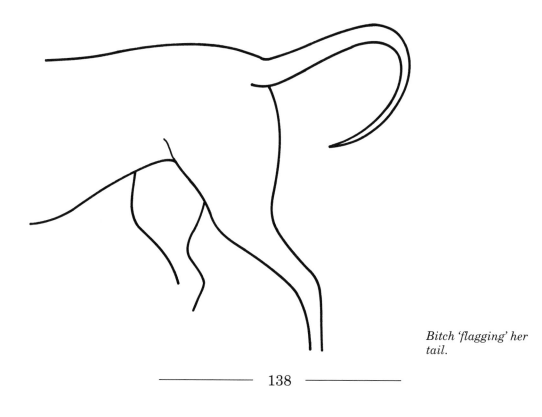

Bitch 'flagging' her tail.

but for the most part the lurcher will need a little more time than, say, a Labrador or a terrier.

If you know your bitch well, she will give you plenty of warning before she comes into season. Most have a marked temperament change, becoming scatty, lacking concentration, sometimes being disobedient, or losing quarry that they would normally have caught. She will scent-mark frequently when out, and may become fractious with other dogs. This behaviour can start as long as six weeks before the season proper, thereby giving you plenty of warning. Use this time wisely to flea and worm her thoroughly, and if a vaccination booster should fall during her season or pregnancy, have her done early rather than let her immunity lapse. Do not, however, do all this at the same time, as it will be too much of a physical strain for her to cope with all this chemical invasion at once. Let at least five days elapse between each treatment, or you will risk permanent damage.

If you can, introduce dog and bitch well before her season, so that they know each other, perhaps play together, and are friends. Before you dismiss this as anthropomorphic nonsense, I can assure you that matings are always easier with animals that like each other – if they hate each other on sight, this is unlikely to change even when the bitch is on heat, and it gives you time to find a stud that is more to her liking. Some bitches will not tolerate a dog around their back end at any time, and I own one such, but because I had taken the trouble to let her meet her prospective mate well in advance, a mating was achieved that was not only trouble-free but evidently very enjoyable to both. She still will not tolerate other dogs around her rear end!

Coming Into Season

The season commences with what is called 'showing colour', when the vulva drips blood-coloured fluid. This can be scant or lavish, depending on the bitch, and some keep themselves so clean that it is easy to miss this first stage. Within a few days, the vulva will start to swell and the bitch will attract male dogs, but she will usually snap at any that attempt to mount her. Do not take any risks, but keep her well away from all canine males, even those which have been castrated. Though these cannot breed, some will attempt to mate, and a few can even achieve a tie, which may introduce infection to the bitch. Throughout the season, whether I have a bitch mated or not, I dose her with tincture of Echinacea, either in her water or 2ml twice daily syringed into her mouth, to reduce the risk of infection in the womb.

A bitch is usually ready to stand for mating at between nine to fourteen days, but this does vary and bitches have been known to conceive at any time during the oestrus period. When ready to mate, she will have little discharge from the vulva, which will be much enlarged, and what discharge there is may be straw-coloured rather than the early-season red. She will turn her rump and 'flag' her tail when approached from behind by another dog, or often even by her owner. The flagging of the tail consists of lifting it and turning it to one side; if you gently touch your bitch's flank just in front of the hindleg, and she flags for you, she is ready to stand. At this time, her desire is very great, causing her perhaps to be restive and whinge a lot. Be patient with her, for the pull of her hormones is very strong and she cannot help it. If left unmated, the season should progress for around twenty-one days, during the last week of which the vulva will shrink back to normal size. For at least one more week, she will remain attractive to male dogs; after that, she will return to normal, and you can stop skulking and hiding and getting up at five o'clock to exercise her. Some bitches experience a false pregnancy which is very convincing, with enlarged nipples, swollen abdomen and coming into milk. A few even exhibit nesting behaviour and spend three weeks or so guarding a bed full of toys or imaginary puppies. Just leave her be, for when these phantom pups are 'weaned' at three weeks or so, she will rejoin the real world again. If, however, she comes heavily into milk, keep a good eye on her in case of mastitis, which we will discuss presently.

Wall-eyed merle; must not be bred to another merle.

Taking Your Lurcher to Mate

But you want her to have a real pregnancy, not a false one, so at some time when she is ready to stand, you must take her to be mated. It is normal practice to take the bitch to the dog, for the dog will be more relaxed on his home ground. If you own a dog that someone wants to put over their bitch, do not let the dog go unaccompanied. Assume that the world is full of thieves and charlatans, and you won't be far wrong. If the stud goes out of your sight, there is no limit on the number of bitches he may be put to, he may be used for poaching while away from you, or you may not get him back at all. If yours is the bitch, go with her. Unless you are using the services of a commercial kennel where there is a wealth of experience and a good reputation at stake, be with her for the mating, for if the dog you have chosen will not mate, she may be put to another without your knowledge.

Accidents happen as well – I used to be involved in racehorse breeding, and remember a well-bred mare producing a skewbald foal because the pony 'teaser' had got at her. If the foal had been whole-coloured, the chances are that nobody would have known, and the same applies with your lurcher. If you are there at the mating, you will know just what has happened. A little biology here – the bitch ovulates a group of 'eggs', each one of which is fertilized separately. It is therefore possible for her to carry pups from more than one sire, if she is mated by different dogs during her season. So once she has been mated to the dog of your choice, do not let her near any other male dog during her period of fertility, for if she stands for him, she will hold service to him as well.

It is this feature that gave rise in the past to the assumption that once a pedigree dog has borne a litter to a different breed, she will breed mongrels ever after, even if mated to a pedigree of the same breed. This is a ludicrous but enduring myth, and my Mother was once given the most beautiful Alsatian bitch that had mis-mated and was going to be shot, as she could supposedly never breed pedigree Alsatian pups again. So, as you don't want a mixed litter, guard your bitch like the jewel she is, and don't let anything else mate her before or after the service from the dog that you have chosen. One more piece of myth-exploding, and I apologize to those of you who cannot believe it, but there are still people who think that dogs operate an incest taboo. Your bitch will cheerfully mate with close relatives, brothers, father, sons, whatever, so do not let her near *any* male dog while she is receptive.

The Event Itself

Agree the terms of the stud fee in advance, and do not be surprised if the stud dog's owner wants the money up front. You can, after all, always return money if the mating does not take place, but the mating cannot be negated if the owner of the bitch does not pay up! The usual rate is the price of a pup or the pick of the litter after the bitch owner has had his or her choice. Allow plenty of time for the mechanics of mating. If you have had a long journey, let the bitch relax, unwind and empty herself before she sees the dog. Never, ever allow an unsupervised mating, no 'chuck them in a shed and go and have a cup of tea' because you won't know what has happened or not happened, and there is a strong risk of either or both dogs being

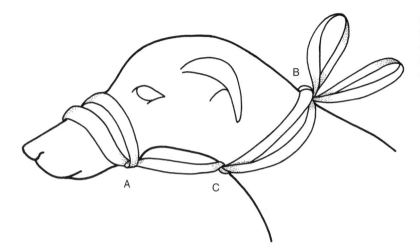

Soft bandage used as muzzle prior to a bitch being mated. Single knot at A and B, double at C.

The mating, dog and bitch of compatible size.

injured, sometimes fatally. There is sometimes a risk of you being injured, too, and it is as well to be prepared to muzzle the bitch, although I have never found it necessary.

In a straightforward mating, dog and bitch will flirt for a while, with much mutual grooming, until the dog judges the bitch to be receptive. This is where tactful human intervention is needed, gently restraining the bitch with an arm around the chest while the dog moves behind her to mount her. She may try to swing her quarters, in which case it is the bitch who must be repositioned, not the dog, who is more easily discouraged. A male dog who is respectful of his owner may instantly defer to him if touched, for only the Alpha pack male may mate. Ideally, you want one person at the front of the bitch, and one supervising the union, and if any adjustments are to be made, move the bitch's vulva not the dog's penis. The moment of penetration can be painful for some bitches, and the bitch may scream or even bite, which puts the person at the front in a risky position – hence the wisdom of muzzling if you are unsure of your bitch's reaction. A simple bandage muzzle tied over the bitch's jaws is fine and less distressing than a rigid muzzle, which also hurts if it should smack you in the face.

The dog is often not fully erect until penetration, so as long as he is in the right place, just hold the bitch steady for him. He will make rapid pelvic thrusts, during which time he is ejaculating, and then show signs of wanting to turn. Let him, for this is the tie, during which he continues to ejaculate. The bitch's ring of muscle

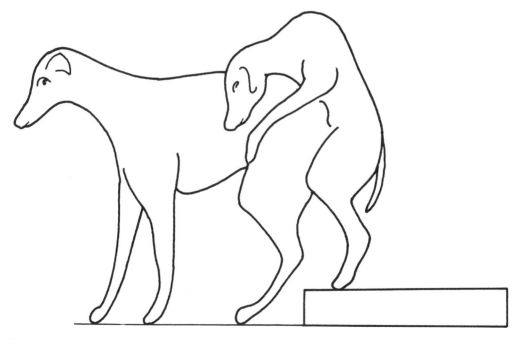

The mating, small dog on large bitch, dog on secure raised platform. The bitch should always stand on level ground to avoid injury to her back.

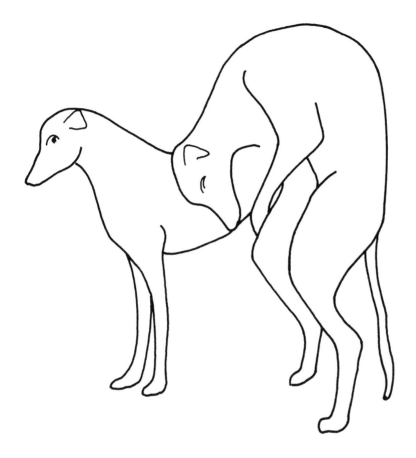

The mating, large dog on small bitch. The bitch may be on raised platform, or dog standing in hollow.

The tie.

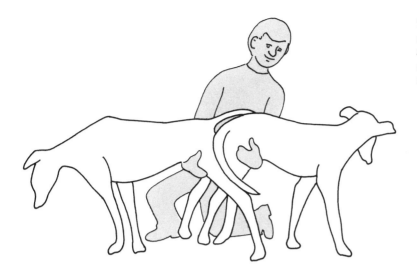

The tie with human intervention, gently supporting the dogs until they release naturally.

around the vulva has now clamped tightly onto the dog's swollen penis, and neither is physically able to disengage. Some bitches scream and struggle violently, and the best method of restraint is to hold both sets of hindquarters together, one arm round each set of hindlegs, and presently the bitch will quieten. If there is a height discrepancy between the dogs, make allowance for it, and be sure that you are sitting comfortably, for the average length of tie is twenty minutes, though it can be as long as forty. During this quiet period, the dog is still ejaculating, but presently the fertile part of the ejaculate is superseded by fluid that does not contain sperm, but washes them deep into the bitch. The two dogs will progressively relax and then part, and the mating has finished.

Afterwards, don't bother with the old kennelman's method of splashing cold water on the bitch's vulva, or even, heaven help us, applying a handful of nettles to it, for the semen has long gone on its journey, and the fluid that leaks from the bitch and is cleaned up by both dog and bitch is not fertile and does not have to be retained. It is possible for pups to result from a mating where the tie does not take place, for the bulk of the fertile ejaculate comes before the tie, but it is certainly better if dog and bitch tie, for the ova are in the uterine horns, not in the womb, and that is where they will be fertilized, implant and develop, which is why they need such a powerful flood of fluid to carry them there. The dangers of leaving dog and bitch unsupervised include the bitch savaging the dog on penetration, rupture to the dog and damage to the bitch if she struggles during the tie, and the possible fracture of the dog's penile bone. One mating is usually sufficient, but if dog and/or bitch are old, or one has a history of low fertility, I would suggest a daily mating until the bitch refuses to stand.

Now put the dog back in his kennel and the bitch safely in your car, and go and have that cup of tea. You have earned it.

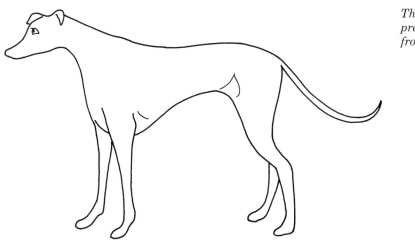

The bitch before pregnancy, seen from side.

The Pregnancy

Do I have to tell you not to work your bitch? Yes, people have worked bitches all through their pregnancy, but it loses many a litter and having gone to all this trouble, it seems a stupid risk. The fertilized ova do not implant for a few days and can be lost, and your bitch is now flooded with hormones and preparing herself for her pregnancy. Exercise her as normal for the first five weeks; feed her as normal, too, for extra rations at this time will lead to big pups and a difficult birth. Don't waste money on having her scanned, for if she is not pregnant it will not make her pregnant, and if she is you will find out soon enough.

It is, however, well worth following a specific worming programme with a wormer that is safe to use during pregnancy, such as Panacur, keeping absolutely to the instructions. During pregnancy, encysted dormant roundworms in the bitch become activated, travel down each placenta and infest the pups. A puppy worming routine will rid them of active roundworm, but a proportion will encyst in turn. In male dogs, this is where they stay, but in a bitch, when she becomes pregnant, the roundworms activate and another generation of pups is born worm-ridden. Worming the bitch throughout pregnancy will not eradicate the roundworms completely, but will certainly cause a marked reduction in them and be very beneficial to the pups. (I am sorry if you are reading this while eating your breakfast!)

If her birthing quarters are different

The bitch before pregnancy, seen from above.

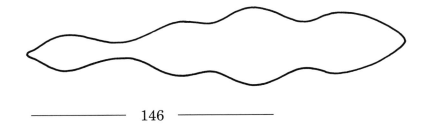

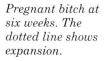

Pregnant bitch at six weeks. The dotted line shows expansion.

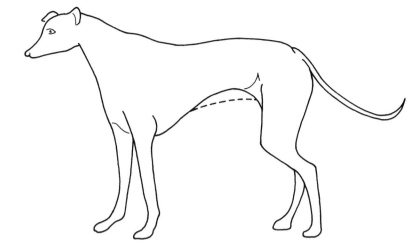

from her normal ones, introduce her now to this new place. Birth is a messy business, so is rearing pups, and you should plan her maternity area with this in mind. She will need a whelping box that is sufficiently bigger than she is to allow her to stretch full length, and with high enough sides to let her in and out but not the pups, which will have long legs one day. Bitch rails are a necessary precaution; some bitches are very careful with their pups, but some are unbelievably clumsy and will squash them to death. She should have sufficient space in her quarters so that she can lie near the whelping box and keep an eye on her babies, but she will not want to go far from them to begin with. Once they are weaned, she will want to get well away from them, and they will need a lot of playing space, so their home for the first

three weeks may well be different from your puppy rearing area. For now, you will want easy access for both yourself and your bitch, a source of light and power, a heat lamp and a floor that is easily cleaned. Now is a good time to start saving newspaper, and get all your friends to do so as well, for you will find yourself using a forest of paper. The puppy box should be clear of the ground but not so high that a whelp can get trapped underneath, and should have a sliding door in one side. It should be made of something that will withstand chewing, and be free from paint or chemicals. If you can persuade your bitch to start sleeping there now, she may agree to give birth there. You must live in hope.

At about the sixth week, the bitch will start to look pregnant, though you may

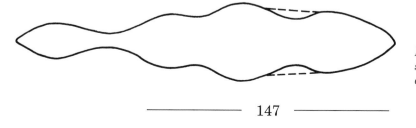

Pregnant bitch at six weeks, seen from above.

have noticed temperament changes. All of mine have suffered morning sickness in the first week. From now until the birth, your bitch will be processing increasing amounts of waste from the unborn pups, so step up the amount of vegetable matter that you feed in order that she can rid herself more easily of these toxins. She will need extra food now, so feed to appetite, and feed often, for she cannot hold a lot of food in one go now that she is full of puppies. I would recommend twice daily through the sixth week, rising to four times from seventh to ninth, but give her more as she needs it. At this time, she will be unable to go through the night without emptying herself at least once, so make arrangements for this. A normally clean bitch will be very distressed at having to foul her quarters, so be prepared to put yourself out a little during this short phase, either by taking her out or leaving a door open for her. By the eighth week, she will be very uncomfortable, and the pups will be easily seen and felt under her skin. I have found that if you rest a hand gently on her abdomen in different places, pups will squirm towards it, and you can get some idea of how many are on board. Research indicates that human babies *in utero* are sensitive to all sorts of stimulus, and it is likely to be the same with puppies. There is a profound wonder in this gentle caressing of the unborn, and the bitch seems to like it as well. New whelps, unseeing, unhearing, will snuggle into my hands as soon as they are born and licked dry, so maybe they remember being

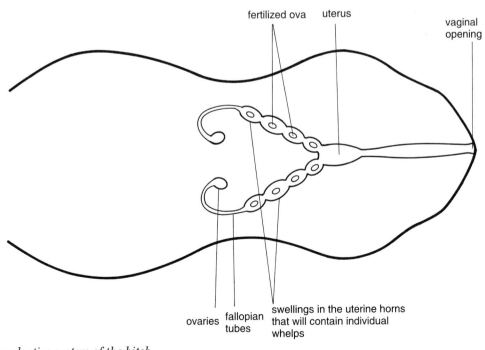

Reproductive system of the bitch.

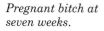

Pregnant bitch at seven weeks.

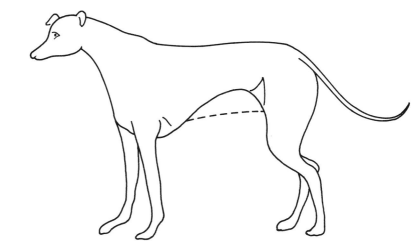

touched through their mother's skin. Or maybe it is just fancy. Perhaps one day we will know.

The Birth

The average length of pregnancy is sixty-three days, but a few days either side can be quite normal, especially if the bitch was mated several times. Make sure that your vet is someone in whom you have confidence, and give plenty of advance warning of the expected due date. If your bitch has whelped before, she will give more precise warning of what is going on than if she is a first-timer. Some like to be left alone, holding back the birth until you leave her for a moment, whereas some desperately want you to stay with them. Go with what she wants, but if yours is a 'leave-me-alone' type, check her regularly and often, in case of complications.

Early signs will be a great restlessness and scratching about, during which your carefully-chosen whelping quarters may be rejected out of hand. No matter how much she wants to give birth in a scrape that she has dug under the ferret hutches, or on your bed, gently return her to where you have chosen. You will see her abdomen ripple with the contractions, and as the birth becomes imminent, the scratching and digging behaviour may become quite frantic. Some bitches, however, do not display any nesting behaviour at all, so put your faith in the contractions, which are beyond her control. She may vomit

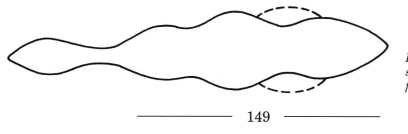

Pregnant bitch at seven weeks, seen from above.

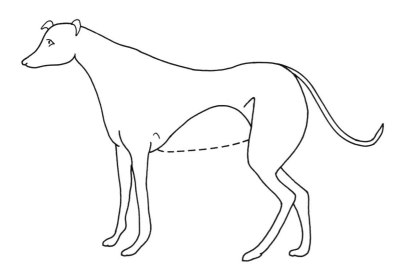

Pregnant bitch at eight weeks, back beginning to dip, wrists beginning to sag.

now, or at any time during the labour. Presently, she will lie down, raise her tail and push out a bag of membrane and water from her vulva, which will prepare the way for the pups. The first whelp may arrive soon afterwards, or you may have another hour to wait. If it takes longer, or your bitch seems to be in distress beyond the panting and straining of a normal birth, get help at once. Sometimes the first pup is very big or can be wrongly presented, and easing him out (it is almost always a male) is a job for experienced hands.

Longdogs can also suffer from uterine inertia either at the beginning of labour or part-way through it, and then help is needed in the form of a pituitary hormone injection such as oxytocin, so if everything seems to come to a stop and your bitch appears to be in distress or looks like she has given up, she must have veterinary assistance. Vets would rather be called too early than too late; my own are so good that I was ensconced in the ante-room with my bitch, a pot of coffee and a pile of magazines, to await results after the injection, and I am sure that it was due to this sensitive treatment that the bitch was spared having a Caesarean.

Each whelp arrives in a welter of mucus and birth fluid, contained in its own membrane and attached to its own placenta. The birth normally ruptures the membrane, with the bitch completing the job. She will nip off the umbilicus and eat the placenta and membrane – let her, this is normal behaviour and must be

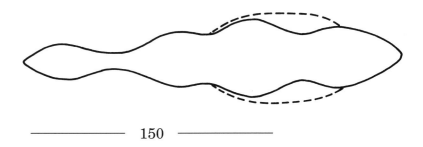

Pregnant bitch at eight weeks, seen from above.

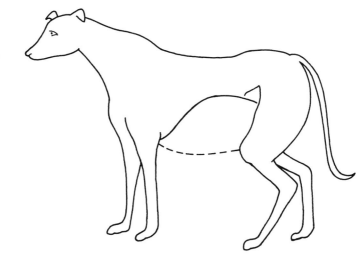

Pregnant bitch at nine weeks, back dipped, wrists and hocks under duress.

allowed. It is over in seconds, though it sometimes looks as if she is going to eat the whole pup, and then she licks her new baby dry and tucks him under her to feed. You will be wanting to find out the sex and colour, but be patient, for it will still be the same sex and colour in half an hour or so, when the next one pops out. When the bitch is busy with the newest arrival, you can look at the others. Check limbs, count toes, open the tiny mouth and check for cleft palate, and then leave the mite alone. If there are obvious deformities, discreetly remove it while the bitch is occupied. Newborns can squeal their indignance very loudly, and if your bitch is distressed by this, leave the handling until later.

After several pups have arrived, your bitch will be desperate to go out and empty herself, so accompany her and watch her closely in case another one pops out. She will appreciate a warm drink, and then be frantic to return to her babies and get on with producing the rest of them. Your job is to remove soiled newspaper and replace with clean as much as you can; don't be precious about it, just remove the worst of the filth. When it looks as if everything is over, take the bitch out for another empty, offer more to drink, and then leave her to suckle her babes in peace. Some people make much of weighing and measuring newborns before they suckle, because they lose their running-dog shape once they

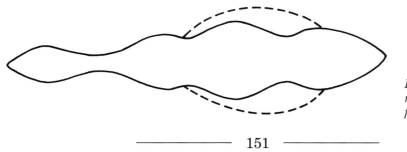

Pregnant bitch at nine weeks, seen from above.

have plumped up on milk, but really this is not a help to the bitch, and I would advise that you keep to a supporting role.

Now that the birth is complete, move bitch and pups onto clean bedding. I recommend an extremely thick layer of newspaper and a large pad of the fleece bedding known as Vet-Bed. This is easy to wash, quick to dry and unlikely to suffocate tiny whelps in a way that is only too easy with straw or hay. Never use shavings; they can clog tiny mouths and choke pups to death. Now leave your lady in peace, and go and get some rest yourself, for that will be in very short supply for the next few weeks.

Litter Size

Lurchers tend to have very large litters, a dozen being commonplace, and sometimes more. Although it is possible to raise litters of this size, the strain on your bitch will be enormous, especially if she is one of the very maternal ones. You also have the problem of finding homes for the other pups, and although many people may have expressed interest when you took your bitch to be mated, you will find that they vanish like snow in summer once the litter is on the ground. If you have pups booked, I recommend that you take a substantial deposit with the booking. Genuine buyers will not object, and you don't need the other sort. Of course, you should return the deposit if, for instance, you do not have the sex that the buyer specified, or cannot otherwise provide what they want.

If you are going to cull your litter, it is best done as early as possible. The longer you leave it the harder it gets, for the bitch, the whelps and the person carrying out the task. I find that five pups are plenty for a bitch to rear, and quite enough to home. If you are keeping one back for yourself, and the stud dog's owner is having one, then that leaves you three reliable new owners to find, which is not too difficult. Culling a litter is a wretched business, and best

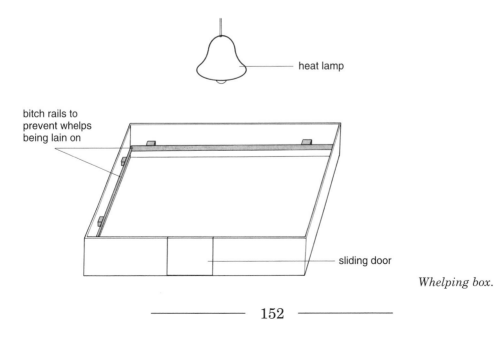

heat lamp

bitch rails to prevent whelps being lain on

sliding door

Whelping box.

Three weeks old – still suckling and very active. Pups mainly Saluki / Greyhound with some Deerhound and Collie a long way back.

done as soon as possible. How do you choose which to keep? First of all, see if there are any which are malformed. The bitch will probably reject these anyway, and she may well take a real dislike to one of the others. Respect her judgement: there may be something wrong with it that will not manifest itself until much later. If one pup is continually being pushed out of the nest, take it away. If it is one that you particularly like, you might be tempted to hand-rear, and that is up to you, but I

Same litter at four weeks.

would always say that if the bitch doesn't want it, go with her decision.

Next, I dispose of any white ones. They grow up into pretty dogs, but are extremely difficult to home. Personally, I have no prejudice against white dogs, but most lurcher owners would not agree with me, and unless you have a specific order for a white pup, then these should go. Equally with pied dogs: some people love them, but they are not generally popular. Then go by sex: it is currently easier to home bitches than dogs, so cut down on the dogs unless you have been especially asked for one. If you still have too many, then go by size: most people like a working dog between 22in and 26in (56–66cm) so if any look much bigger or much smaller than the others, and are likely to mature outside these sizes (take an educated guess based on the size of the parents), then take them away. Remember that a bitch will tend to mature slightly smaller than a dog. If any whelp really appeals to you, really has something about it, trust your instincts and keep it, regardless of size, sex or colour. If it has that much charisma at a few hours hold, then it is likely to be something special.

Week One

Assuming that the birth is over, and the litter is now a suitable size for rearing, your bitch is comfortable in her quarters, with a heat lamp on if necessary, you can almost relax. This is not, however, a time to leave the bitch for long periods and go back to work. She must be checked hourly, for there is much that can go wrong. Some bitches have a tremendous maternal instinct and look after their pups beautifully; others are lousy mothers and seem hell-bent on squashing their pups, ignoring their desperate cries. Some will not suckle their pups, and some pups must be coaxed to suckle. A very few bitches do not bond with their pups, especially if they have had a difficult birth or even a Caesarean, and you will have to explore the world of hand-rearing. Sometimes a bitch will expel a dead pup several days after whelping the litter, and then she must be taken to the vet at once in case other dead pups are stuck inside. If she is put on a course of antibiotics, then the pups will be suckling antiobiotics in their milk, which may make them ill, although this is less likely with more modern antibiotics. The bitch will be cleansing from

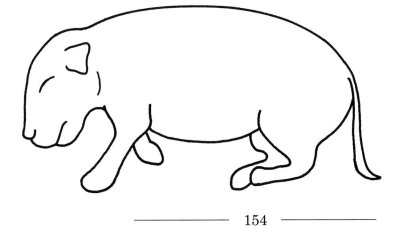

Whelp in first week. Blunt mouth and nose set back for suckling, front legs much more developed than hindlegs. Ears and eyes sealed. Can crawl using front legs.

her uterus, and the discharge may be copious, bloody, or brown. This can go on for quite a few weeks, and again must be monitored. At the first sign of foul smell or unusual colour, she should be checked by your vet. Raspberry Leaf tablets are a great help in cleansing at this time.

There is attitude to take into account, too: some bitches are very litter-proud, and will not suffer their pups to be handled by any other than their owner. Go with her wishes; this is an occasion when even the sweetest bitch can attack a human and do some damage, and it is perfectly understandable. Never allow unsupervised children to see the whelps, and do not allow either children or adults to handle them if the bitch is touchy. She may not even pause to rumble a warning if she feels her babies are being threatened. Humans like to pick puppies up, but it frightens the pups and can damage them, so even if your bitch is happy to share her puppies, veto any picking-up tendencies, and instead tell people to get on the floor with the whelps.

During the first week, whelps are blind and deaf, but their senses of smell, touch and taste are well developed. They are very vocal and surprisingly active, able to shuffle about by pushing themselves along with their hindlegs, and have to be checked and counted frequently, so that they do not get stuck under something and perish. The bitch's water bowl should be away from the puppy box, so that they cannot fall in and drown, and her food bowl must be removed as soon as she has finished eating. She will be ravenous at this time, consuming around four times her normal ration, which should be divided into four to six feeds per day. If she wants more, give her more. Her normal diet will be fine, just more of it. Do not make the mistake of

giving her milk just because she is producing it, for it will just make her scour (suffer from severe diarrhoea). Her bowels will tend to be loose anyway because of the hormonal changes and because she is clearing up after the puppies. She will suffer from the most appalling flatulence, and need to go out to empty herself very often. I once shared a room with a bitch for the first three weeks after whelping, and as it was a winter litter I was unable to open the window for fresh air. The evil-smelling miasma of sulphurous fart took some surviving, and it is a measure of just how much I cared for this bitch that I was able to endure it. It certainly alters your perspectives when you have a hot longdog snuggled up to you, leaking milk, post-birth fluid and methane. Just as well she is one of your best friends.

Complications

Eclampsia
One of the most serious complications that can arise after giving birth is eclampsia, and it will kill your bitch very quickly. It is a metabolic disturbance caused by her blood calcium levels being depleted too far by the production of milk for her pups. It is not a lack of calcium, but a breakdown in the ability to convert it that causes the problem, so a well-fed bitch nursing a small litter is as much at risk as the hungry bitch with a big litter.

Eclampsia comes on very quickly: the bitch will tremble and pant, developing a stiff-legged, tottering gait, and if left untreated, will collapse and die very quickly. At the first signs of panting and staggering, the vet must be called out, as this is an emergency. The condition is quickly rectified by injection of calcium borogluconate, but the bitch must be closely monitored for any recurrence, and it may be necessary to take the pups off her and rear by hand. The first three weeks of rearing are the danger period for eclampsia, and some bitches are much more prone to it than others. A natural diet with plenty of raw meaty bones will help to protect against this condition; there is some indication that it is linked to an iodine deficiency, in which case a daily Kelp tablet may help to prevent it. Do not supply iodine in any other form, as pure iodine is toxic. If your bitch develops eclampsia symptoms, you may only have half an hour in which to save her, so call out the vet as soon as you suspect something is wrong.

Mastitis
This is an inflammation of one or more of the mammary glands. The bitch will obviously be reluctant to suckle, and the affected teat(s) will be hot, hard, purplish-red and painful. She will probably have a raised temperature. First-aid at the onset of mastitis is the application of a warm, wet cloth to the affected area, but if it does not respond fairly rapidly, then antibiotics are needed. Not only is mastitis unpleasant for the bitch, it may cause her to snap at the pups when they try to suckle from the painful teat. If left untreated, the place could ulcerate, so rapid intervention is necessary.

Hand-Rearing

You might, for various reasons, be left with a litter of pups to hand-rear. This is incredibly tiring and not to be undertaken lightly. To begin with, they will need feeding every two hours, and you will need to stimulate their bladders and bowels after each feed by gently stroking their tummies with a warm, wet cloth – your vet will show you how. There are good bitch-milk substitutes available, but if at all possible the pups should have their first feed from the bitch, for then they will have taken in the valuable colostrum, the first milk, which is full of protective antibodies. If this is not possible, then there are colostrum substitutes available as well. Your vet will be able to help with all this, as well as supplying suitable feeders. Everything that you use must be kept very clean, and the pups should be in a moist atmosphere under a heat lamp. Sufficient humidity can be achieved by having a damp towel in the puppy box and a bowl of water in the puppy room. Even if it is summer, the heat lamp must be on, for the tiny bodies chill very quickly.

Hold the pups slightly upright to feed, so that they do not choke, and do not overfeed. As they have no mother to lick them clean, mop up any dribbled milk before you attend to the other end, and make sure both ends are clean and dry when you return them to the puppy box. Hand-reared pups tend to be more advanced than the conventional sort, and you will be able to wean them quite quickly once their teeth start coming through at the third week. I reared seven pups by hand once; luckily they had mother's milk available although she would not suckle them – a traumatic Caesarean meant that she refused to bond with them; if I had had the vet then that I do now, the crisis would never have occurred, but this all happened a long time ago. I weaned the litter on plain yoghurt, raw mince and comb cappings from a local beekeeper, and they grew into fine lurchers. It put years on me, however, and I still remember the relief when they went onto four-hourly feeds and I could actually get some sleep.

Fading Puppy Syndrome

This is sometimes also known as 'Flat Puppy Syndrome', as the pups lose condition quickly and look flat instead of plump. This heartbreaking condition can be the result of any one of several infections brought into the puppy area by visitors or from the bitch. A litter of apparently healthy puppies can simply fade away and die within days. Obviously call your vet if this starts to happen, and to prevent it, be very strict with hygiene, insist that visitors wash hands and remove shoes before going into the puppy room, and never allow visiting dogs.

Dewclaws

It used to be common to remove the dewclaws of running dogs, the reason given being to avoid damage in later life. This is a very old-fashioned view, but still persists in some areas. If you go coursing with Greyhounds, you will see that every

dog has its dewclaws left on, and while stopper pads often sustain damage, dewclaws rarely do. There is some evidence that the dewclaw assists the dog in turning, and my own dogs use their dewclaws like thumbs, to hold onto things. I would never remove dewclaws, for it is my belief that their use far outweighs their disadvantage, and my dogs, which are worked hard, do not suffer dewclaw injuries.

Week Two

At about ten days old, the pups' eyes will start to open. Very young pups will have blue eyes and be unable to focus, and at this stage the eyes are very weak. It is very important that the pups are not exposed to strong light at this time, which could damage their sight. Whereas other breeds can spend their lives with defective eyesight and their owners would probably never know, a gazehound cannot work to its full potential unless its vision is perfect. If your pups are still under a heat lamp, then the light that is put out by it along with the heat could prove harmful, and I

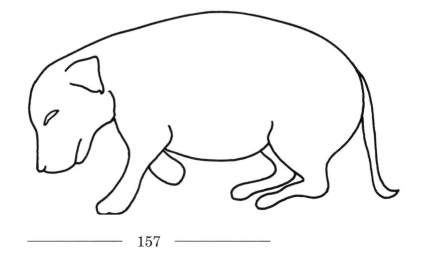

Whelp in second week. Eyes and ears begin to open at around ten days. Nose profile begins to lengthen in preparation for teeth. Hindlegs a little stronger, and able to assist crawling.

suggest that you change to a nursery heater until the eyes have turned brown. Adult eye colour takes some weeks to establish, and may go through several colour changes. A light-eyed dog is traditionally unpopular, while 'wall' and 'moonpie' eyes are regarded with superstition by some. All work equally well, and I would never discard a dog for her eye colour, but if it really offends you, don't keep that dog for your own. You will be looking at her for years, so you might as well pick one that pleases your own eyes.

Trimming the Nails

Round about the end of the second week you will need to trim the pups' nails, as they will soon grow to sufficient length to cause the bitch discomfort. Two-week-olds can be real wrigglers, and if you can get help, do so, for the job is not easy and the supply of nails seems endless. Sharp nail scissors are quite adequate for the job; use blunt-ended ones if possible to avoid accidentally hurting the puppy. Check your bitch's nails too, in case the lack of exercise means that they have become too long for comfort.

I find that by the second week, the bitch is ready to leave her pups for longer spells, and will be keen to come for short walks with you. Against this, you have to balance the need to avoid bringing infection back to the pups. There is no easy answer for this one: I tend to take the bitch out and keep away from areas that are very 'doggy', but this is not possible for everybody. The bitch is always so much more cheerful after a short break from her duties that I believe it does more good than harm, but you will have to decide this one for yourself.

Fleas and Ticks

In summer, fleas and ticks will find their way onto your puppies, and must be removed before a serious infestation results. One preparation, 'Frontline', is marketed as being safe for very young pups, and certainly works very well, but I try and avoid chemicals for as long as possible, and you may prefer just to go over them with a flea comb. Ticks on puppies are easily loosened by covering the tick with soft margarine or butter, which is completely safe for the puppy and suffocates the tick. After leaving the buttered tick for five or ten minutes (make sure that the other puppies do not lick off the butter), twist it anticlockwise to remove it. If the bitch is kept clean, and the puppy box likewise, you should be able to cope well enough with the occasional parasite.

All through week two, the pups' hearing will be developing as their ears unseal, and their hindlegs will be strengthening so that they are very mobile indeed. Considering that lurchers are silent in adulthood, they are amazingly noisy puppies, and you will be used to conversation from the puppy room by now. Any problems will be announced by sharp yells, which should bring you running. I am always fascinated by the noisy dreams of tiny whelps who have been nowhere and done nothing – of what do they dream? One of mine howled like a timber wolf on his second night of separate life, an unnerving noise from something that looked like a small plush bag. Tiny whelps will benefit from gentle stroking, but should not be picked up unless it is unavoidable. It is lovely to see them shuffle towards your hands when you place them in the puppy box, and very humbling when you see how much they want to be friends.

Whelp in third week. Eyes fully open but sight not well developed. Ears functioning. Milk teeth beginning to cut through gums. Can toddle for short distances.

Week Three

Weaning

This is when the teeth come, but before that can happen the blunt guinea-pig faces have to lengthen a little, though they are a long way from the pointed sighthound snout that you will see one day. Eyes still do not focus too well, but legs are getting less rubber and more wire, and the little ones will be toddling. The arrival of teeth means that the bitch will be less eager to suckle, and the youngsters will be easing their gums on anything hard – her legs, your fingers, the sides of the puppy box – so now is a good time to introduce real food. If your bitch is a jealous feeder, it is prudent to feed her away from the pups now. The natural way of weaning is for the bitch to regurgitate her own food for the pups, who receive it in a pleasingly warm and partly digested state. This can be a queasy experience for humans, and can also mean that the bitch goes short of food because she is taking it all to the pups. If your bitch is determined, it is easier to go with the flow and let her get on with it, making sure that she has plenty of food for herself, because the phase will only last a week or two at most. However, if it really is repugnant to you, then you can take her out of the room for her own food and don't let her back in to the pups until the best part of an hour has elapsed, by which time her meal will be sufficiently well digested to stay down. Meanwhile, you can place a shallow dish of food outside the puppy box, and release the monsters by removing the sliding door. Place them around the dish and watch them paddle through it, fall in it, get covered in it and do everything except eat it. They will complain bitterly, and want some nice milk (this happens when the bitch regurgitates for them as well).

What should you place in the puppies' dish? Every dog book that you read will tell

The independent pup grows into an independent dog.

you something different, but as long as the food is sloppy, it won't be long before some of it starts going inside the puppies. I use minced raw meat, plain yoghurt and gravy made from bone stock (not from a packet or jar, which will be full of salt and artificial flavourings). Let the bitch back in, and she will hoover up the left-over puppy food and wash her sticky children. Then take everything away before it gets fly-blown. Flies are a penance with a summer litter, and cold is a problem with a winter one, so you cannot win. Put food down for the pups four times daily, and always feed outside the nest, because now that they are on solids, what comes out will be solid as well, and the bitch will not be so keen to clean up after them. If you feed outside the nest, they will empty themselves outside too, and will be well on the way to being house-trained. Even very tiny pups will struggle off their Vet-Bed to empty on the newspaper, and if they are allowed to be clean, they will be. I have never house-trained any of my homebred puppies as they have always made strenuous efforts to be clean.

Worming

Towards the end of the third week, the puppies will need to be wormed. I find a liquid wormer can be easily syringed into their mouths, but an extra pair of hands is always a help. Worm the bitch on the same day as well. Although you will not see the results of the bitch's worming, because modern wormers destroy the worms' protective slime and the adult dog can then digest them, puppy digestions are not strong enough, and they will pass quantities of live worms. You will have a hectic time clearing up after them, because the shortest time interval known to Man is that between a puppy emptying itself and then dancing in it. Do not touch the worms with your bare hands, disinfect the area very thoroughly with a disinfectant that is safe around young animals, and wash and disinfect your hands. Dispose of the wormy droppings by burning them, because roundworms and their eggs are great survivors, and will live in soil for years. You are in any case about to enter a new world of waste disposal, for the pups will be producing amazing amounts of waste, which is technically clinical waste, and if you live somewhere where you do not have the luxury of a bonfire, you will soon be developing a haunted expression as you try to dispose responsibly of sack after sack of mucky newspaper.

Your pups will also be ready to move from their baby quarters to somewhere such as a kennel and run, because their legs are working pretty well by now, and they need space in which to exercise them. The bitch will still want to spend time with them, but will also need to get away from them when they become too persistent. Therefore the new quarters should offer her access to a 'safe' area where she can keep an eye on them but also escape when she needs to. Lurcherman Dave Sleight had a Kelpie cross bitch who used to climb up the weldmesh of the kennel sides and hang up out of reach, but that's Kelpies, and a more con-

ventionally bred bitch would prefer an easier option.

Week Four

Teeth are well through by now, and the pups will be completely weaned, though many bitches continue to suckle. Feed the pups before letting the bitch in, so that they take less milk and the bitch can start to dry off. She will probably be looking rather a wreck by now, even though you have fed her well. 'Milking off her back' the farmers call it, and her hip bones will protrude like an old milch cow's, her topline will have gone and she will be ribby. It is not unusual for her coat to fall out, which is hormonal, so don't worry. Just give her lots of meat and vegetable matter, and you can give the pups the same. As well as the liquidized vegetables, they will enjoy chewing on carrots and other hard vegetables (not potato), and will be able to demolish raw chicken wings and slices of breast of lamb. You will have discovered a new use for an old baby-gate, as an avalanche of puppies will descend upon

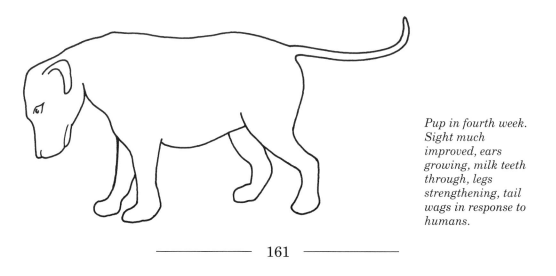

Pup in fourth week. Sight much improved, ears growing, milk teeth through, legs strengthening, tail wags in response to humans.

you every time you enter the kennel, and getting out alive will be a challenge.

Homing the Puppies

Have you chosen your puppy yet? It is time to advertise the others, or, if you rely on word of mouth, to shake up the grapevine. People who have ordered puppies should now come and pick theirs; you have the advantage, as you have been closely involved with the litter and know their individual personalities. When people come to view the litter, only let them see the pups that are available for sale, otherwise you may get a hard time from somebody wanting the one that has been chosen by you or the stud dog owner. Stick to your price – it is usual to sell dogs more cheaply than bitches, and to add on a charge if people want their pup to be vaccinated. You will, however, be keeping the pups for a few weeks yet, so to reduce the aggravation from timewasters, take a deposit on every proposed sale. If people haggle over the price, send them away. Your pups have been reared with every care, and are worth the price that you have set. Hagglers are often the sort to sell a pup on at a profit, and that is not the sort of fate for which you have reared them. Be very careful about admitting strangers to your home, or revealing that you have a litter of lurcher pups, for it is not unknown to have whole litters stolen and maybe the bitch as well. Taking precautions makes the litter that much more difficult to sell – I did advise you not to breed lurcher pups – but is better than putting in all that work and then losing everything.

Once you have chosen your own pup, start to separate her from the rest of the litter to stay with you for short periods of time. Let her play around and with you,

feed her from your hands, let her curl up next to or on you and sleep. This will bond her to you, which is the first link in the 'golden thread' that runs between the best dogs and the best owners. At first, she will be worried at being away from her littermates, so only keep her with you for a very short time before putting her back in the world that she knows. Soon she will be eager to come out and be with you, and you can spend perhaps half an hour together at a time. Upon her return, she will experience a status change with her siblings, so leave enough time to settle her into the nest again before you leave them. This is also a good time to put a soft collar on her, but be sure to remove it when she goes back into the nest, or the other pups will drag her around by it, causing injury to her and to them.

Week Five

Time to worm the pups again, for they must be wormed every fortnight until they are thirteen weeks old. Do not worm them when they are just about to have their vaccinations, or have just had them, but otherwise they must have that wormer through them regularly. Worming by syringe ensures that every pup gets the correct dose, and you will find that they struggle much harder at five weeks than at three! You will probably need to cut nails again, too, although the pups are very active now and, if their run has a concrete floor, they may be wearing their nails down satisfactorily. They should be fully weaned, and able to deal with chunks of raw meat and raw bones, but still feed the vegetable gravy and yoghurt gruel as well. The bitch may or may not still be suckling; let her do what she wants. She will not want to be confined with the pups at all, but will choose to pop in and visit them several times daily. Some pups are mature enough to leave home at five weeks, but few owners are experienced enough to care for such a very young puppy, and it is best to keep them for a little longer. If prospective owners have chosen a pup and are eagerly waiting for it to be old enough to leave home, they can usefully introduce their scent to the pup by bringing an old towel or cotton T-shirt that has been in their bed for a week and become well scented. Leaving this towel in the puppy box will familiarize the pup with the scent of her new family, and then when she leaves home she can take the towel as a 'comforter' because by then it will also smell of puppy nest.

Week Six

In my youth, puppies changed homes at six weeks old, but nowadays people tend to leave it later. Personally, I like a pup to come to me as young as possible, for the next few weeks are critical in terms of puppy development. They are also very demanding at this age, needing lots of stimulus and space, and seemingly endless cleaning out. Sharp milk teeth seem to get at everything, and status squabbles occur frequently. If the new owners are the

Pup in fifth week. Legs arrive! Pup can play vigorously, run and pounce, and interact with people. Muzzle continues to lengthen.

sort who can cope with a pup of this age, and the pup is sufficiently mature, let her go. This will also give the less assertive pups a break, as they will be having something of a hard time by now. Remove the dominant pups, and the others will blossom. Your own pup should be with you as much as possible by now, and may not be living with her siblings at all. Your bitch will be returning to normal, and looking to go out with you as usual. 'Pups? What pups? I'm a working dog!'

Weeks Seven to Twelve

Pups should be leaving home during this period. If you are having the litter vacci-nated, first vaccinations generally take place at nine weeks, and second at twelve, although different vets do work differently. Although few vets will come out to vaccinate puppies now, it is positively dangerous to take your precious litter of pups into the motley infections lurking in the surgery waiting room. A good compromise is if the vet will come out to your vehicle and vaccinate the puppies *in situ*. Have you ever tried to transport a whole litter of squawking puppies? As a damage-limitation exercise, confine them in a cage or box in the back of the car. I can guarantee that they will be sick, and probably other things as well, on the journey. It is a pity that most pups' first car rides end in trips to the vet, as it can take quite

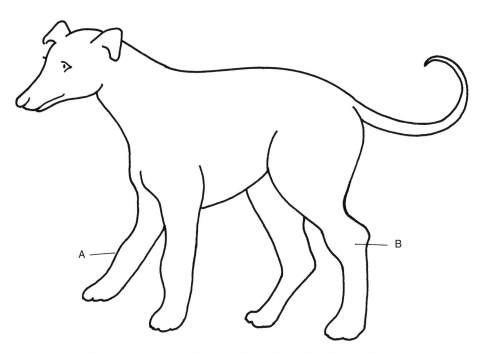

Pup in sixth week. Beginning to look like a lurcher at last. Face fining down, muzzle lengthening in proportion, legs strong and displaying large growth plates A and B. Ready to leave for new home.

a bit of work to persuade them to like car rides afterwards. With your own pup, you can take her out with you prior to the vaccination trips, but of course you cannot let her run about outside without risking infection. Parvovirus and distemper are still major killers of young dogs, and those that survive are often badly damaged. On balance, it is probably better to have some work still to do with car journeys than get this far and have to bury your pup and start again.

With luck, the pups will leave for their new homes quite quickly, and then you will be left to get on with life with your own. In practice, however, it is rarely this smooth: you will be let down, you will discover certain homes are not, after all, suitable, people will ask you to keep pups on while they go on holiday, finish the haymaking, and so on, and you may well be left with an extra pup at a time when you want to be putting work in on your own youngster and getting your bitch fit again. It is often the pup that you least like that stays the longest! But eventually they will have gone, you will have cleaned up, washed and disinfected away all trace of the litter, and put away your heat lamp.

Was it a worthwhile exercise? Think well before you undertake it. If you buy, you should be able to get what you want: if you breed, you have to take what you get. I know people who have bred litters and not had a worthwhile pup to keep, and I recently bred a litter of twelve in which ten were males and of the two bitches, one was born dead and the other, a weak and runty little thing, died soon after. I had desperately wanted a bitch, but had the choice of keeping a dog pup or going without. Your bitch will be months off work, although her working ability will be unaffected once she starts again. Bring her back to fitness with great care and patience, for her body has taken quite a battering. Her seasons may take a year or more to settle down, and the first one after a birth may be a heavy one. If she has had a Caesarean, it would be unwise to breed from her again, and if she was not a good mother, there is no reason to suppose that she would be any different the next time around. If you do want to breed from her again, let her have at least one season before you do so. You will probably need that length of time yourself, to forget all the hard work and worry involved.

CHAPTER 9

THE DECLINING YEARS

A lurcher's working life is relatively short, which is both her tragedy and ours. Assuming that she does not start hard work until she is two, she will be at the peak of her powers for four years or so. After her sixth birthday, her speed will be much reduced, but her quarry sense will support her, and you probably won't see much difference in the catch rate, though you will in the method of catching. For a while, you will be able to pick and choose the lamped rabbits that you send her on, and then her lamping will be over, as will her coursing, but you can still take her bushing and ferreting, or even rough-shooting, as long as she does not get too cold or wet. Old joints and muscles will be susceptible to chill and damp, and she will appreciate a warm coat on winter nights in the kennel, or when riding home in the car after a day of work. She will take longer to recover from a working day, and then have to go onto half-days only. She will require longer to heal after injury, and she will not be able to get as much goodness out of her food.

At this stage of your dog's life it is even more important to keep her fit, and not let her become soft or overweight, though her muscles will not have the firmness and definition that she had in her youth. Check her teeth and clean them if necessary; a dog that gets plenty of raw bones is unlikely to get a general build-up of tartar, but the roots of the canine teeth can need attention. I have never found the commercial toothbrushes and toothpastes for dogs to be of much use, but that may be operator error! A gentle scrape with a thumbnail often does the job on new tartar, though for the really bad stuff, a proper dentist's scraper padded with cotton wool or kitchen paper will do a quick, efficient job. Do pad it, because you don't want an accidental slip to groove the tooth and provide a 'key' for more tartar to cling. Be sure to look at her back teeth, too, and watch for any changes in her gums, which should be pink and healthy-looking no matter how old she is. Check the state of her kidneys by observing how much water she is drinking, and how often she needs to empty herself. Any change in bowel habits is an early warning to you: the biggest killer by far of old dogs is cancer, so be sure to check her over regularly. Mammary tumours are very common in bitches, and an old unspayed bitch runs an increasing risk of uterine infections after her season. Old male dogs must have their genital areas checked, for tumours will occur there, and both sexes run the risk of internal growths. Skin tumours, too, will become common, some of which simply need to be kept under observation, some of which will kill in a matter of weeks. Any lump, or change to an existing lump, must be investigated by a vet as soon as you notice it.

The stresses of a working life will start to show on your dog's physique: she will lose the proud arch over her loins, her back may start to dip, her wrists sag and her toes spread. The texture of her coat will change, and she will be longer about her moulting. Her tear ducts may overflow,

No more coursing, but a fine roughshooting companion.

causing her eyes to run, and she may develop cataracts or become hard of hearing. You may have to lift her in and out of the car, nor will she be able to slide under or leap over obstacles as once she could. Most sadly of all, her mind may become muddled. When I was a child, a dog was lucky to live past its eighth year, but now dogs of twice that age are not uncommon. Now they live long enough to get diabetes, heart trouble, leukaemia, or suffer from senility. And they live long enough to retire.

Bearing in mind that you need time to bring on a pup, this can leave you in difficulties if you wish to continue hunting, and you risk losing your hard-won permission if you take a few years out to let a dog grow old, or a pup come on. One way around that is to have a few hunting partners with whom you can go out regularly, using their dogs once yours is retired, but it is hard for a true dog person to do without an active working dog. Some dogs take their retirement more gracefully than others: one of my old girls is happy to act on a consultancy basis, her gamefinding abilities seemingly unimpaired as she points into covert. She is still canny enough to stand in the rabbit-runs so that she can scoop up a bunny as it flees, but she leaves the bramble-bashing and the coursing to the young entry. She will retrieve shot game that she has found and flushed, and is happy to tag along on most of our outings, though her lamping days are long gone and she no longer has an adequate concentration span for ferreting.

Twelve-year-old dog, still ferreting.

Retired and enjoying the sunshine.

The next in line, who is currently middle-aged, is unlikely to take her waning powers with such tranquillity, but we will cross that one when we come to it.

If you decide to breed from an old lurcher, there are more risks attached than when breeding a bitch in her prime, and a worthwhile consideration is to take one litter from your bitch while she is still young, even though it means losing the use of her for half a year, in order that she may more safely have other litters when she retires. It is no kindness to take a first litter from an elderly bitch, and you could lose both her and the pups. Older lurchers tend to have smaller litters than young ones; even so, I would recommend culling the litter down to two or three as a maximum for her to raise. Older male dogs have less problem breeding, although their sperm is not so good in quality, therefore try to use a young dog on an old bitch, and vice versa.

Having said this, there is nothing wrong in breeding from an elderly bitch as long as you are aware of the pitfalls and give your vet plenty of warning in case you have to bring your bitch in for emergency treatment which will, of course, always be out of hours and probably over a Bank Holiday. If she has had a litter before, she may sail through her confinement, produce and raise a quality small litter which gives her fulfilment and you the satisfaction of carrying on the line. But she will need astute observation and a lot more care than she did at three years old. You will really have to be on the ball for the first few weeks, and it might mean somebody being at home all the time. An aged bitch deserves better than being bred from over and over, although she is likely to enjoy producing one or two families once her working life is done. Do watch out for infections of the uterus that can rumble on for weeks before suddenly erupting into a potentially fatal illness. Any signs of temperature, increased drinking, listlessness

The old lady still enjoys a dip.

or even just 'not being herself' mean that you must get her to the vet. And even if everything goes marvellously well, remember that she will take a long time to recover from the demands of raising even a small litter.

As well as conventional medication, we have a number of alternative aids available to help the old dog in her declining years. Some aches and pains resulting from old age will respond to copper in the collar, or a special medical magnet, and many vets use acupuncture or homeopathy with great success. Sometimes a vitamin or mineral supplement makes the world of difference, but use those made specially for dogs, not for people, as their nutritional needs are different from ours. Access to good meat, fresh vegetables, plenty of grass and herbs is even more important for the elderly dog as her system begins gently to wind down.

But your old lurcher needs her mind as well as her body to be kept sweet, and if you truly do not have the time or the kennel space to continue to give her interest and make her feel worthwhile, then you will have to consider other options. Old lurchers can sometimes be found new homes as family pets, and indeed their quiet, clean ways make them ideal house companions once the need to run has left them. If you do this, please make sure that it is with someone that you know and trust, not the sort to take her out and sell her the following day. Some lurchers bond so strongly with their owners that this is not a kind solution, but neither is it kind to keep an old dog grieving in her kennel while a younger one supplants her. It can be very hard to find the time to take an old lurcher out after working the younger one, and I know many a retired lurcher, once the jewel in her owner's kennel, who never leaves her pen. This is no thanks for a lifetime of good service.

However, if you keep all your retired animals for as long as they remain healthy, as I do, you do end up with an awful lot of them. It is all work and feed

Going home.

bills sometimes, especially as all of my dogs go out on exercise, training or work every day, and I certainly have no quarrel with the owner who opts for a humane end to the old dog's life once her working years are done. This can be a greater kindness than moving her on, or leaving her behind every time you go out, or trying to keep her going when she works her hardest despite the bewilderment of constant failure. Our lurchers give us so much, both in work and devotion, that the final gesture has to be for their well-being and not ours. The choice is entirely yours.

EPILOGUE

The first year of owning your lurcher seems like unremitting hard work, but as you approach the second year it all starts to come together. Your sapling dog and you grow more confident in each other, as she begins to build on the foundations that you have established for her. The rest is down to experience, and she will gain quarry sense in her own time. So long as you have the patience to let her learn, and the understanding that she will miss many, many catches through inexperience, you may be certain that one day she and you will make the very special combination of a working dog and her owner, doing the first and best of all the jobs that dogs have ever done for people. Lurchers being what they are, she will work with you rather than for you, with the dignity of a falcon, and she is better so.

You will not know the exact moment that it all gels until, one day or night, you come back with rabbits in the bag and a lightness of heart, your dog striding at your side with her tail high, knowing how good she is, pushing her nose into your hand and looking at you with her great, laughing eyes. You realize that you have not spoken a word to her in all the time you have been out, yet she has gone where you wanted her to and found, coursed and held, over and over. She has ignored the sheep, jumped or gone through as told, done her work with silent efficiency, and come straight back to hand. You are a team. Welcome to the world of the working lurcher.

RECOMMENDED READING

Billinghurst, Dr Ian, *Give Your Dog a Bone* and *Grow Your Pups With Bones* (published by the author, 1998)

Cavill, David, *All About Mating, Whelping and Weaning* (Pelham Books, 1987)

Elliott, Mark and Pinkus, Tony, *Dogs and Homeopathy, the Owner's Companion* (Ainsworth's Homeopathic Pharmacy, 1996)

Portman-Graham, R., *The Mating and Whelping of Dogs* (Popular Dogs Publishing/Century Hutchinson, 1986)

The Countryman's Weekly (published weekly by *The Countryman's Weekly*, Yelverton, Devon PL20 7PE)

USEFUL ADDRESSES

National Lurcher and Racing Club
39 St Mary's Gate
Chesterfield
Derbyshire S41 7TH

Ainsworths Homeopathic Pharmacy
36 New Cavendish Street
London W1M 7LH

The Countryside Alliance
The Old Town Hall
367 Kennington Road
London SE11 4PT

INDEX

Alsatian *see* GSD
antibiotics   122, 154, 156
arnica   120, 124, 125

barbed wire   13, 42, 112
bedding   108–8
Bedlington
  lurcher   13, 80, 87
  terrier   50, 136
birth   149–52
bitch, dog or   21–2
bitza lurcher   18–19
Bull Terrier lurcher   17–18, 80

calcium borogluconate   156
cattle dog lurcher   18, 89
choke chain   33, 55
collar, electric shock   54–5
Collie
  Bearded   8–9, 16
  Bearded Collie lurcher   11–12
  Border   81, 136
  Border Collie lurcher   10–11, 37, 66,
    89
colour   24–5
commands   27–8
copper toxicosis   136

deer   15
  fallow   82
  muntjac   82
  red   82–3
  roe   82
  sika   82–3

Deerhound   37, 51, 71, 80, 82, 83, 136
  lurcher   14–15, 99
dew claws   157
dislocation of joints   124–5

eclampsia   155–6
eggs, feeding of   98
entering to quarry
  deer   81–4
  feather   86
  fox   77–81
  hare   84–5
  mink   87
  rabbit   59–77
  squirrel   86–7
eyes, pups'   157–8

feeding   89–100
ferreting   59–60, 73, 110
First Aid   119–22
fox, suitable dog to work   13, 15, 18, 20,
    137
fractures   124

gamekeepers   110–11, 113, 117, 126
Greyhound   8–9, 17, 19–21, 37, 71, 80, 84
GDS (German Shepherd Dog)   82, 141
  lurcher   12
guarding instinct   16, 18
gun, working with   60–1, 73
gundog lurchers   16–17

herbs   96–7
hand-rearing   156–7

hand signals   27
hard mouth   50, 52–4, 57, 60, 80, 137

jumping training   40–3

kennel or house   24, 30–1
killing mouth   13, 23, 52, 60

lamping   59–70, 110
lead training   32–3
leptospirosis *see* Weil's disease
livestock, steadying to
  cat   46–7
  cattle   45
  horses   45–6
  sheep   43–5
Lurchersearch   131, 133–4

mating   138–45
marking of buries   74
mastitis   156
milk fever *see* eclampsia

nails   102, 106, 158, 162
neutering   21, 105

opening up   50–2, 57
over-running   125–6

pack behaviour   31–2, 71–2, 102
parasites
  fleas   87, 127, 158
  mange   127
  ticks   127–8, 158
  worms   93, 97, 127, 146, 160–1, 162
poisoning, accidental   118–19

Police, liaison with   114–15
poulticing   121
pregnancy   126–7, 146–9
  false   101, 105, 140

rats   87
recall training   36
retrieving   23, 37–40, 136

Saluki   51, 71
  lurcher   15, 19, 31, 80, 82, 84
season, oestrus   116–17, 139–40
slip, use of   68
sprains and strains   123–4
stud fee   141

teeth, care of   166
Terrier, working with   72–3
theft   129–34, 162
toes, damage to   19, 106–7
tumours   166–7

vaccinations   139, 164–5
vet, choice of   120

water
  drinking   100–1, 118
  training to   47–9, 104
weaning   159–61
Weil's disease (leptospirosis)   87
whelping box   146, 152
Whippet   12, 14, 15, 18, 20–1, 37, 51, 71, 80, 94
whirrier   14
whistle, training to   27, 49, 67
working weight   104–5